Credit and General GERMAN

The National Qualifications Examination Papers and the
Scottish Certificate of Education Examination Papers
are reprinted by special permission of
THE SCOTTISH QUALIFICATIONS AUTHORITY

ISBN 0 7169 9335 x
© Robert Gibson & Sons, Glasgow, Ltd., 2000

ROBERT GIBSON · Publisher
17 Fitzroy Place, Glasgow, G3 7SF.

CONTENTS

Part 1997
WEDNESDAY, 28 MAY
11.05 AM – 11.50 AM

GERMAN
STANDARD GRADE
General Level
Reading

When you are told to do so, open your paper and write your answers **in English** in the spaces provided.

You may use a German dictionary.

Marks

You are staying with your German pen friend. One morning you look at a magazine your friend has helped to produce at school.

1. There is a crossword puzzle in the magazine. Here are some of the answers to the crossword.

1. | N a s e |

2. | F r e i t a g |

3. | K i n o |

4. | F r ü h l i n g |

5. | B e i n |

6. | M i l c h |

7. | A |

8. | Z |

Here are four of the clues for the crossword. Which are the correct answers from the list above? Write the correct number in the box opposite each clue. **(4)**

	Answer Number
Sitzt in der Mitte vom Gesicht	
Eine der vier Jahreszeiten	
Hier kann man Filme sehen	
Letzter Buchstabe im Alphabet	

Marks

2. There is an article by a girl called Michaela. She writes about the advantages
    of having a computer at home.

Ich habe vor einem Jahr einen Computer zum Geburtstag bekommen. Mit
dem Computer zu schreiben ist einfach. Meine Hausaufgaben schreibe ich
jetzt alle mit dem Computer. Wenn ich Fehler mache, gehe ich einfach
zurück und übertippe den Fehler.

Tick (✓) **two** of the boxes to show whether the following statements are **true** or
false.

(2)

	True	False
Michaela bought the computer with her pocket money.		
She does all her homework on the computer.		

Marks

3. You see this advertisement for a local hotel.

Verbringen Sie einen schönen Urlaub im

Landhaus Haake

_____

Genießen Sie die ruhige Lage auf dem Land.

Viele schöne Wanderwege, teils durch den Wald, in der Nähe.

_____

Winterangebot bis 30. April 1998

3 Wochen wohnen
2 Wochen bezahlen!

_____

Wir freuen uns auf Ihren Besuch

(*a*) Why would people want to go to this hotel? Write **two** things.   **(2)**

_____

_____

(*b*) What special offer is the hotel making for the winter?   **(1)**

_____

Marks

4. A girl called Margarete talks about a part-time job she has at McDonald's.

Ich arbeite schon seit zwei Jahren bei McDonalds. Ich bin einfach hingegangen und habe gefragt, ob 'was frei ist, und sie haben gesagt, okay, fang bei uns an.

Wir sind ein gutes Team. Vier an der Kasse, vier in der Küche. Seit sechs Monaten bin ich jetzt Schichtführerin. Das heißt, ich bediene nicht mehr die Gäste. Ich passe nur auf, daß alles gut läuft.

(*a*) How did Margarete manage to get the job at McDonald's? **(1)**

_____

(*b*) How has her job changed in the last six months? Write **two** things. **(2)**

_____

_____

5. This article gives some tips for a healthy life-style.

Zum Fit- und Gesundbleiben gehört gesundes Essen.
Das heißt:

- Zuviel Alkohol soll man vermeiden. Er hat viele Kalorien und kann zu schweren Krankheiten führen.

- Zuviel Salz und salzige Nahrungsmittel sind ungesund.

- Nicht viel Zucker essen. Süßigkeiten machen dick. Frisches Obst oder Obstsaft ist besser.

- Nicht rauchen! Rauchen schadet dem ganzen Körper; es macht die Haut grau und führt oft zu Lungenkrebs!

According to the article, why should we avoid the following things? Give **one** reason for each.

(4)

Too much alcohol	
Too much salt	
Too much sugar	
Smoking	

Marks

6. These young people were asked: do you like living in Germany or would you prefer to live in a different country?

Ceyda

Ich würde lieber in der Türkei leben. Da ist es wärmer, und da wohnen mein Opa und meine Oma. Deutschland gefällt mir, aber nicht so gut wie die Türkei.

Kurt

Ich würde lieber in Italien wohnen. Da kann man im Winter gut Ski fahren. Es gibt überall in den Bergen Sesselbahnen. Es macht Spaß, damit hochzufahren.

(*a*) Ceyda and Kurt would prefer to live in another country. Why? **(4)**

	Would prefer to live in . . .	Why? Give **two** reasons for each.
Ceyda	Turkey	1. 2.
Kurt	Italy	1. 2.

Marks

Sascha

Es gefällt mir gut hier in Deutschland. Man hat hier gute Arbeitsmöglichkeiten, und ich habe nette Freunde in der Schule.

(*b*)   Sascha likes living in Germany. Why?   **(2)**

	Likes living in . . .	Why? Give **two** reasons.
Sascha	Germany	1. 2.

7. Three young people talk about what they do to protect the environment.

Marks

Thomas

• Ich tue, was ich kann. Auch meine Familie. Wenn wir durch den Wald wandern, nehmen wir Tüten mit und sammeln den Abfall auf.

• Wir bringen auch unsere alten Kleider zu einer Sammelstelle.

Ecki

• Ich fahre so wenig wie möglich Auto. Meiner Meinung nach liegt das Hauptproblem bei den Autoabgasen.

• Ich werfe auch kein Papier auf die Straße.

Susanne

• Bei uns zu Hause trennen wir den Hausmüll—Aluminium, Altpapier und Plastik.

• Für die Schule kaufe ich nur Hefte aus Altpapier.

What do they do for the environment? Write **two** things for each person.

(6)

Thomas	
Ecki	
Susanne	

Marks

8. Here are your pen friend's answers to a questionnaire in the magazine. The questionnaire is about how energetic or how lazy people are. (Your friend's answers are the ones marked with a cross.)

Bist du energisch oder faul?

1. Dein Freund hat dich für den Abend eingeladen. Er wohnt fünf Kilometer von dir entfernt. Wie kommst du zu ihm?

  (*a*) Deine Mutter fährt dich mit dem Auto hin und holt dich abends wieder ab.   ☒

  (*b*) Die ganze Strecke ist gut beleuchtet. Du fährst also mit dem Fahrrad zu deinem Freund.   ☐

2. Es regnet, und du mußt zur Schule. Meistens gehst du den Weg zu Fuß. Was machst du heute?

  (*a*) Du sagst deiner Mutter, daß du krank bist. Du gehst heute nicht in die Schule.   ☐

  (*b*) Du ziehst eine Regenjacke an und gehst trotz des schlechten Wetters zu Fuß.   ☒

What is the first situation described in the questionnaire?	
What would your pen friend do in this situation?	

What is the second situation described in the questionnaire?	
What would your pen friend do in this situation?	

(4)

[END OF QUESTION PAPER]   **Total (32)**

1998
TUESDAY, 26 MAY
G/C   9.15 AM – 10.00 AM
F/**G** 10.00 AM – 10.45 AM

GERMAN
STANDARD GRADE
General Level
Reading

When you are told to do so, open your paper and write your answers **in English** in the spaces provided. You may use a German dictionary.

Before leaving the examination room you must give this book to the invigilator. If you do not, you may lose all the marks for this paper.

You are staying with your German pen friend. One day you read a magazine.

1. In the magazine there is a competition. You have to guess the countries from the clues that are given. Here are the clues:

A

• Das Land grenzt an die Nordsee.

• Hier kann man am Markt bekannte Käsesorten kaufen.

B

• Das Land liegt auf einer Insel.

• Alle Autos, Lastwagen und Busse fahren auf der linken Straßenseite.

C

- Das ist das größte Land Europas.

- In der Hauptstadt sieht man diesen berühmten Turm.

D

- Aus diesem Land kommen die besten Uhren.

- Viele Urlauber kommen zum Wandern und Skilaufen hierher.

Choose **one** clue for each country and say what the clue is.

		(4)
A Holland		
B Great Britain		
C France		
D Switzerland		

2. This article is about how much money different groups of people spend on holidays.

Singles reisen teurer

Was die Deutschen pro Person für eine zweiwöchige Urlaubsreise ausgeben.

Jugendliche	**1069DM**
Junge Erwachsene	**1311DM**
Singles	**2266DM**
Paare	**1792DM**
Familie mit Kindern	**1026DM**
Familie mit Jugendlichen	**1499DM**
Rentner	**1548DM**

Put a tick (✓) in the correct box to show whether these statements are **True** or **False**. **(2)**

	True	False
Families with young children spend more than families with teenagers.		
Pensioners spend least of all.		

Marks

3. This article is about open-air cinemas.

> ## *Filme unter freiem Himmel*
>
> Open-air Kinos sind in!
>
> Hier ein paar Tips, damit das open-air Kino noch mehr Spaß macht.
>
> ** Kissen mitbringen, aber bitte keine Stühle: Die sind nur im Weg.
>
> ** Picknickkorb nicht vergessen! Getränke und Würstchen gibt es fast überall, sie sind aber meist viel zu teuer.
>
> ** Einen Regenschirm braucht man auch. Ohne Regenschirm bei strömendem Regen macht keinen Spaß.

Tick (✓) **three** pieces of advice given in the article.   **(3)**

	Tick (✓)
Bring a chair to sit on.	
Wear warm clothes.	
Bring a cushion to sit on.	
Bring an umbrella.	
No umbrellas—they block the view for other people.	
Bring something to eat and drink.	

4. This article gives four tips for dealing with wasps.

Marks

Die 4 goldenen Wespen-Regeln

1. Wespen lieben Cola-Dosen und dunkle Flaschen! Vorsicht beim Trinken!

2. Im Herbst nicht barfuß im Garten gehen. Zu dieser Zeit liegen die Wespen oft auf dem Erdboden!

3. Wespen hassen Zitronen! Legen Sie einfach eine Scheibe Zitrone auf das Fensterbrett, und die Wespen kommen nicht zu Besuch!

4. Versuchen Sie niemals, Wespennester selbst zu zerstören!

Choose any **three** of the tips and say what they are.

(3)

(*a*) _____

_____

(*b*) _____

_____

(*c*) _____

_____

Marks

5. Three young people write about a proposed ban on rollerblading in city centres.

Dieter

Ich finde Rollerblading sehr gefährlich in der Stadtmitte. Ich denke, zum Beispiel, an die Fußgängerzone. Man kann dort ältere Menschen sehr leicht überfahren.

Barbara

Inline-Skater bringen Leben in die toten Innenstädte und Fußgängerzonen. Mir macht es einfach Spaß, lautlos durch die Straßen zu gleiten.

Lisa

Ich fahre schon seit einem Jahr und bin noch nicht mit einem Fußgänger zusammengestoßen. Ich passe immer gut auf, wenn ich fahre. Ich finde es viel besser als mit dem Bus oder Auto zu fahren.

(*a*) Why is Dieter in favour of the ban? **(1)**

_____

_____

(*b*) Barbara and Lisa are against the ban. Why? Give **one** reason for each of them. **(2)**

Barbara: _____

_____

Lisa: _____

_____

Marks

6. In the magazine there are suggestions of games you could play on a long car journey. They are guessing games.

> ■ Welche Farbe hat das nächste Auto, das uns überholt?
>
> ■ Wie viele Leute sitzen im Auto hinter uns?
>
> ■ Mit welchem Buchstaben beginnt das Kennzeichen des nächsten Autos?
>
> ■ Ist der nächste Fußgänger auf der Straße Mann oder Frau, Junge oder Mädchen?

Choose any **three** of the games and explain clearly what they are. **(3)**

(a) _____

_____

(b) _____

_____

(c) _____

_____

Marks

7. This article is about three young people and the sports they play.

CHRISTINE

Seit zwei Jahren schwimme ich in einem Verein. Mindestens zweimal die Woche trainiere ich, manchmal sogar viermal. Aber nur, wenn nicht zu viele Hausaufgaben zu machen sind. Hinterher bin ich immer sehr müde.

ANDREAS

Turnen mag ich am liebsten. Mit meiner Turngruppe nehme ich oft an Wettkämpfen teil. Dreimal habe ich schon den ersten Platz gemacht. Eine Medaille gab's auch! Wer turnen will, muß ein bißchen Mut haben.

MARIANNE

Ich spiele gern Fußball mit den Jungen. Wir spielen gegen andere Mannschaften. Manchmal verlieren wir, aber das macht uns nichts aus. Ich gehe jeden Samstag zu einem Fußballspiel. Dort schaue ich mir die Profis an, und probiere hinterher, was ich gesehen habe.

Write **one** name in each box to answer the questions.

(3)

	Name
Who tries to copy the experts?	
Who finds the training quite hard?	
Who has won competitions?	

8. In this article some young people say what they are worried about.

Marks

Was macht dir angst?

Martina

Ich war eine Zeitlang im Ausland und jetzt verstehe ich mich mit meinen Freunden nicht mehr. Ich fühle mich jetzt ziemlich alleine.

Axel

Ich finde es schlimm, älter zu werden. Am liebsten würde ich nie älter als dreißig sein.

Hassan

Ich kann mir nichts Schlimmeres vorstellen, als den ganzen Tag im Büro zu sitzen und einen Job zu machen, der mir überhaupt keinen Spaß bringt.

Ilka

Manchmal habe ich Angst vor der Zukunft. Alles ist so ungewiß: Beruf, Wohnort, Geld und vieles andere.

What are these young people worried about? Write **one** thing for each person.

(4)

Martina	
Axel	
Hassan	
Ilka	

9. You read the headlines from four articles in the magazine.

Marks

1.

Traumjob Ärztin
→ Aber wie sieht das Studium aus?

2. **MEDIZIN**

Kopfschmerzen hat jeder ab und zu—was hilft dagegen?

3. **Plötzlich bekommt das Leben eine neue Bedeutung**

Karolina, 16, erbt ein Schloß

4. „Danke schön, und bis zum nächsten Mal!"
Jugendliche bringen Hilfsgüter nach Rußland

Choose any **three** of the headlines and explain clearly what the articles are about.

(3)

Headline Number	

Marks

10. One evening you go to a restaurant with your pen friend for a meal. After the meal you are asked to fill in this questionnaire.

Restaurant »Zum Spieß«

IHRE MEiNUNG ist uns wicHTig!

1. Wie oft kommen Sie zu diesem Restaurant?

☐ erstmalig   ☐ mindestens einmal pro Woche

☐ mehrmals im Jahr   ☐ mehrmals im Monat

2. Wie ist Ihre Meinung nach dem heutigen Besuch?

	zufrieden	unzufrieden
über das Essen	☐	☐
über die Bedienung	☐	☐
über den Preis	☐	☐

This is the first time you have been to this restaurant. You find the food is good, but the service is slow and the meal is too expensive.

(*a*) Give your answer to the first question by putting a cross in the correct box. **(1)**

(*b*) Give your answers to the second question by putting a cross in **one** box in each row. **(3)**

Total (32)

[END OF QUESTION PAPER]

GERMAN
STANDARD GRADE
General Level
Listening Transcript

Transcript—General Level

> **Instructions to reader(s):**
>
> For each item, read the English **once,** then read the German **twice**, with an interval of 7 seconds between the two readings. On completion of the second reading, pause for the length of time indicated in brackets after each item, to allow the candidates to write their answers.
>
> Where special arrangements have been agreed in advance to allow the reading of the material, those sections marked **(f)** should be read by a female speaker and those marked **(m)** by a male: those sections marked **(t)** should be read by the teacher.

(t) You are going with your pen friend, Thomas, to visit his cousin, Gisela, in Hameln.

(f) or (m)   **Du fährst mit deinem Brieffreund Thomas nach Hameln. Dort besucht ihr seine Kusine Gisela.**

(t) Question number one.

Thomas tells you how you are going to get there. Part of your journey will be by train.

Tick **two** of the boxes to show which other forms of transport you will use.

(m)   **Wir müssen mit der U-Bahn Linie 10 zum Hauptbahnhof fahren. Dann geht's mit der Bahn weiter nach Hameln. Dort holt uns meine Kusine Gisela mit ihrem Auto ab. Sie fährt uns dann zu ihrer Familie.**

(30 seconds)

(t) Question number two.

Thomas wants to buy a present for his aunt.

What **two** suggestions does he make? Tick **two** of the boxes.

(m)   **Wir müssen meiner Tante etwas mitbringen. Sie liest gerne. Ich glaube, ich kaufe ihr etwas zu lesen. Oder wir können ihr etwas Süßes zu essen kaufen, eine Schachtel Pralinen vielleicht?**

(30 seconds)

(t) Question number three.

You arrive at the station. Thomas asks about the train times to Hameln.

Tick the correct departure time and platform.

(m)   **Der nächste Zug nach Hameln fährt gleich um 10.45 Uhr von Gleis 7 ab. Sie müssen sich aber beeilen.**

(30 seconds)

(t) Question number four.

As you head for the train you hear the following announcement.

Why does someone have to go to the information desk?

(f)
or
(m)
Achtung! Achtung! Ein schwarzer Koffer ist auf Bahnsteig vier gefunden worden. Wer diesen Koffer verloren hat, soll sich bitte an der Information am Eingang des Bahnhofs melden. Danke!

(30 seconds)

(t) Question number five.

You arrive in Hameln. Thomas's cousin, Gisela, meets you.

Put a tick at the **two** places Gisela must go to on the way home.

(f) **Hallo, ihr beide. Also, auf geht's nach Hause! Zuerst muß ich noch an der Tankstelle vorbei. Mein Benzin ist fast alle. Ich muß aber auch zur Apotheke. Für Vati soll ich Medikamente abholen.**

(30 seconds)

(t) Question number six.

Gisela tells you about where she lives.

Write **three** things she says.

(f) **Wir wohnen auf dem Land. Es dauert ungefähr zwanzig Minuten, bis wir da sind. Das Haus liegt direkt an einem schönen, kleinen See. Dort kann man prima angeln gehen.**

(30 seconds)

(t) Question number seven.

You arrive at Gisela's house and meet her mother. She welcomes you.

Gisela's father is a doctor.

Where is he? What has happened?

(f) **Herzlich willkommen hier bei uns! Ich hoffe, ihr hattet eine gute Reise. Mein Mann kommt erst später nach Hause. Er ist Arzt und mußte schnell in die Stadt zu einem alten Patienten, der im Haus gefallen ist.**

(30 seconds)

(t) Question number eight.

Gisela's mother takes you to meet her other daughter, Ingrid.

What is Ingrid doing?

(f) **Komm mit! Ingrid ist im Garten. Sie deckt den Tisch für das Abendessen. Wir wollen heute abend draußen essen.**

(30 seconds)

(t) Question number nine.

Gisela discusses her plans for the evening.

What are her plans? Write **two** things.

(f) **Ich gehe heute Abend ins Kino. Es läuft zur Zeit ein toller Abenteuerfilm. Habt ihr Lust mitzukommen? Danach treffe ich mich mit meinen Freunden in der Stadtmitte.**

(30 seconds)

(t) Question number ten.

That evening you meet Dieter, one of Gisela's friends.

He tells you about his plans for after the summer holidays.

What is Dieter planning to do? What **two** things does he ask you?

(m) **Hallo, ich habe gerade gehört, du kommst aus Schottland. Nach den Sommerferien werde ich für drei Monate eine Schule in Edinburg besuchen. Wohnst du weit von dort? Können wir uns vielleicht an einem Wochenende treffen?**

(30 seconds)

(t) Question number eleven.

Later that evening you talk about what you are going to do the next day. Gisela has some ideas.

What does she suggest doing if the weather is good? Write **two** things.

(f) **Ich weiß nicht, wie das Wetter morgen wird. Wenn es schön ist, können wir eine Radtour machen. Wir haben Fahrräder. Wir können auf dem Land ein Picknick machen.**

(30 seconds)

(t) Question number twelve.

What does she suggest doing if it is wet? Write **two** things.

(f) **Falls es regnet, können wir immer noch ins Einkaufszentrum gehen. Ich brauche ein paar Hefte für die Schule. Dann könnten wir ins Heimatmuseum gehen. Das ist ganz interessant.**

(30 seconds)

(t) Question number thirteen.

Gisela tells you what her friend Dieter has arranged for Saturday evening.

What has been planned? Write **two** things.

(f) **Samstagabend sind wir um 6.00 Uhr bei meinem Freund Dieter zum Abendessen eingeladen. Er hat außerdem noch Karten für das Theater. Wir werden das Theaterstück „Der Rattenfänger von Hameln" sehen. Das wird bestimmt Spaß machen!**

(30 seconds)

(t) End of test.

You now have 5 minutes to look over your answers.

[END OF TRANSCRIPT]

1998
TUESDAY, 26 MAY
11.45 AM – 12.10 PM
(APPROX)

GERMAN
STANDARD GRADE
General Level
Listening

When you are told to do so, open your paper.

You will hear a number of short items in German. You will hear each item twice, then you will have time to write your answer.

Write your answers, **in English**, in this book, in the appropriate spaces.

You may take notes as you are listening to the German, but only in this paper.

You may **not** use a German dictionary.

You are not allowed to leave the examination room until the end of the test.

Before leaving the examination room you must give this book to the invigilator. If you do not, you may lose all the marks for this paper.

Marks

You are going with your pen friend, Thomas, to visit his cousin, Gisela, in Hameln.

Du fährst mit deinem Brieffreund Thomas nach Hameln. Dort besucht ihr seine Kusine Gisela.

1. Thomas tells you how you are going to get there. Part of your journey will be by train.

   Tick (✓) **two** of the boxes to show which other forms of transport you will use.   **(2)**

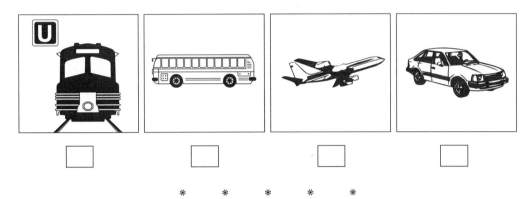

   *   *   *   *   *

2. Thomas wants to buy a present for his aunt.

   What **two** suggestions does he make? Tick (✓) **two** of the boxes.   **(2)**

	Tick (✓)
Flowers	
A bottle of wine	
A book or magazine	
Biscuits	
Chocolates	

   *   *   *   *   *

3. You arrive at the station. Thomas asks about the train times to Hameln.

   Tick (✓) the correct departure time and platform.

   (a) Departure time: 10.45 ☐   11.15 ☐   11.45 ☐   **(1)**

   (b) Platform: 5 ☐   7 ☐   9 ☐   **(1)**

   *   *   *   *   *

Marks

4. As you head for the train you hear the following announcement.

Why does someone have to go to the information desk? **(1)**

_____

*   *   *   *   *

5. You arrive in Hameln. Thomas's cousin, Gisela, meets you.

Put a tick (✓) at the **two** places Gisela must go to on the way home. **(2)**

	Tick (✓)
Library	
Petrol Station	
Supermarket	
Chemist	
Baker	

*   *   *   *   *

6. Gisela tells you about where she lives.

Write **three** things she says. **(3)**

_____

_____

_____

*   *   *   *   *

7. You arrive at Gisela's house and meet her mother. She welcomes you. Gisela's father is a doctor.

(*a*) Where is he? **(1)**

_____

(*b*) What has happened? **(1)**

_____

*   *   *   *   *

8. Gisela's mother takes you to meet her other daughter, Ingrid.

What is Ingrid doing? **(1)**

_____

*   *   *   *   *

9. Gisela discusses her plans for the evening.

What are her plans? Write **two** things. **(2)**

_____

_____

*   *   *   *   *

10. That evening you meet Dieter, one of Gisela's friends.

He tells you about his plans for after the summer holidays.

(*a*) What is Dieter planning to do? **(1)**

_____

(*b*) What **two** things does he ask you? **(2)**

_____

_____

*   *   *   *   *

11. Later that evening you talk about what you are going to do the next day. Gisela has some ideas.

What does she suggest doing if the weather is good? Write **two** things. **(2)**

_____

_____

*   *   *   *   *

Marks

12. What does she suggest doing if it is wet? Write **two** things.
(2)

_____

_____

✳   ✳   ✳   ✳   ✳

13. Gisela tells you what her friend Dieter has arranged for Saturday evening.
What has been planned? Write **two** things.
(2)

_____

_____

✳   ✳   ✳   ✳   ✳

Total (26)

[END OF QUESTION PAPER]

GERMAN
STANDARD GRADE
General Level
(Optional Paper)
Writing

When you are told to do so, open your paper and write your answers **in German** in the spaces provided.

You may use a German dictionary.

Before leaving the examination room you must give this book to the invigilator. If you do not, you may lose all the marks for this paper.

As part of a school project, your class is exchanging information with a school in Germany. Each pupil in your class has a German partner.

Note: Examples are given to help you with ideas. These are only suggestions and you are free to use ideas of your own.

1. You have to write about a typical school day. You could say when school starts and finishes, where you have your lunch, when you do your homework, how much homework you have, etc. Write at least **three** sentences.

2. In this section you ask your partner about school subjects. You could ask what subjects they take, what their favourite subject is, what they don't like studying, what the teachers are like, etc. Ask at least **three** questions.

?

3. Write about the things you do after school and at weekends. You could mention any hobbies or interests you have, what you do with your friends, where you go, etc. Write at least **three** sentences.

4. The German school is planning a visit to Scotland in three months' time. Write about what there is to see and do in your area. Write at least **three** sentences.

5. The German school has sent information on how German teenagers celebrate their birthday. Explain how you usually celebrate **your** birthday. You could say when your birthday is and write about the kind of presents you get, what you do on your birthday, etc. Write at least **three** sentences.

[END OF QUESTION PAPER]

1999
WEDNESDAY, 26 MAY
G/C   9.20 AM – 10.05 AM
F/**G** 10.05 AM – 10.50 AM

GERMAN
STANDARD GRADE
General Level
Reading

When you are told to do so, open your paper and write your answers **in English** in the spaces provided.

You may use a German dictionary.

Before leaving the examination room you must give this book to the invigilator. If you do not, you may lose all the marks for this paper.

Marks

Your German pen friend has sent you her local newspaper and some magazines.

1. A local girl, Katrin Wypior, is "Young Personality of the Week" in the newspaper.

Ich bin fünfzehn und spiele seit fünf Jahren Geige.

Mein Haupthobby ist aber Schwimmen. Klassische Musik höre ich nie. Ich höre lieber Gruppen wie 911.

Mein Traum ist es, eine Weltreise zu machen.

Mein größter Fehler ist wahrscheinlich, daß ich sehr faul bin. Was ich an mir besonders mag: ich komme prima mit meinen Freunden aus.

Katrin Wypior

Complete the grid.　　　　　　　　　　　　　　　　　　　　**(4)**

Name	Katrin Wypior
Age	15
Main hobby	
Favourite music	Groups like 911
Her dream	
Worst fault	
Best quality	

Marks

2. There are some adverts for sports shops in the newspaper.

A

Achtung Sportler!

Große Auswahl an Sport–
bekleidung und Schuhen

Mo. – Fr. 9.00 – 17.00 Uhr
Sa. 9.00 – 13.00 Uhr
So. geschlossen

B

 **Freizeitwelt**

Boote, Bootsmotoren, Wassersport,
Camping, Zelte, Propangas

(So. geschlossen)

C

**Ihr
Sportschuh-
geschäft**

Wir haben geöffnet:

Mo., Di., Do., Fr. 9.00 – 23.00 Uhr
Mi. 6.00 – 23.00 Uhr
Sa., So. 10.00 – 18.00 Uhr

	Letter
Where could you buy a track suit?	
Which shop is open every day?	

(2)

3. You see an advert for a trip to Scotland.

Die Schottland-History-&-Mystery-Tour

1. Tag	Aus Hamburg kommen Sie um 15.30 Uhr in Newcastle an. Sie fahren dann direkt zur schottischen Hauptstadt, wo Sie übernachten.
3. Tag	Tageswanderung (6–8 Stunden) durch das schottische Hochland. Abendessen in einem schönen, alten Schloß.
5. Tag	Sie haben die Möglichkeit, in Inverness einen Einkaufsbummel zu machen. Nachmittags besichtigen Sie einen schottischen Garten.

What do you do on these days? Write **two** things for each day.   **(6)**

Day 1	
Day 3	
Day 5	

Marks

4. In a magazine you find some ideas for different kinds of parties.

Mafia Party

Klamotten:	Schwarzer Hut und Sonnenbrille.
Essen und Getränke:	Italienisch mit Rotwein.
Action:	Mit Wasserpistolen schießen.

Urlaubsparty

Klamotten:	Kurze Hose und Hawaiihemd.
Essen und Getränke:	Grillen und Limo.
Action:	Fahrradtour zum Strand.

Choose any **one** of the parties and say what it would be like.　　**(3)**

What would you wear at this party?	
What would you eat and drink?	
What would you do?	

Marks

5. These young people write what they think about holidays.
Constanze and Franz find holidays boring.

Ich finde Ferien langweilig. Denn ich bin oft
allein zu Hause. Außerdem gehe ich gerne zur
Schule. Da ist immer was los.

Constanze

Ich finde Ferien langweilig. Meine Eltern sind
tagsüber an der Arbeit, und ich muß immer im
Haushalt helfen, abspülen, Essen vorbereiten . . .

Franz

(*a*) Why do Constanze and Franz find holidays boring? Write **one** thing
for each person. **(2)**

Constanze	
Franz	

Marks

Sebastian and Nicola enjoy their holidays.

Ferien sind doch einfach super! Wir fahren als Familie immer nach Spanien. Dort bin ich von früh bis spät mit meinen spanischen Freunden.

Sebastian

Ferien sind fast das Schönste im ganzen Jahr! Ich kann mich ausschlafen und tun, wozu ich Lust habe.

Nicola

(*b*) Why do they enjoy their holidays? Write **one** thing for each person. **(2)**

Sebastian	
Nicola	

Marks

6. This article gives you three exercises for your legs.

Tun Sie mehr für Ihre Beine.

Übung A   Legen Sie sich auf den Rücken, strecken Sie die Beine in die Luft und bewegen Sie die Beine, wie beim Fahrradfahren.

Übung B   Sie legen sich auf den Rücken. Heben Sie die Beine gestreckt etwa zwanzig Zentimeter über den Boden und halten sie so für ein paar Sekunden ruhig in der Luft. Sie legen sie wieder ab und wiederholen die Übung 10 mal.

Übung C   Sie stellen sich barfuß auf die Zehenspitzen und wieder zurück. Nach 10 bis 20 Zehenständen schütteln Sie die Beine aus.

Match the pictures to the instructions. Write the correct letter in each box.   **(2)**

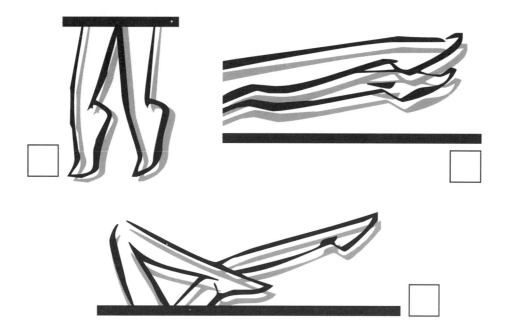

Marks

7. This article is about a phone card Germans can use when on holiday abroad.

.T. . .Card .

Mit der T-Card Holiday von der Deutschen Telekom können Sie in fünfundsechzig Ländern von fast jedem Telefon aus telefonieren.

Die Karte kann man aber auch in Deutschland benutzen.

Die T-Card Holiday gibt's für 25 oder 50 DM, und ist bei der Post zu kaufen.

Only **three** of the following statements are true. Tick (✓) the three statements which are true. **(3)**

	Tick (✓)
You can use the card in 65 countries.	
You can use it for any telephone.	
You can also use it in Germany.	
You cannot use it in Germany.	
You can buy it at the post office.	

Marks

8. These young people say what their idea of beauty is.

Was ist „schön"?

Thomas:	Wie man aussieht, ist nicht so wichtig. Hauptsache, man ist sympathisch, freundlich und hilfsbereit.
Andrea:	Ich trage jeden Tag Make-up und ziehe mich schick an. So bin ich immer guter Laune.
Klaus:	Es ist mir gleich, wie ich aussehe. Man muß mich einfach nehmen, wie ich bin.
Peter:	Ich mag Mädchen mit blonden, kurzen Haaren. Lockiges, rotes Haar finde ich schrecklich.
Wibke:	Leute, die glücklich sind, sind natürlich schön.

Who say the following things? Write the correct name in each box.

(4)

	Name
People must take me the way I am.	
Happy people are beautiful people.	
It's more important to **be** nice than to **look** nice.	
It makes me feel better if I try to look good.	
Hair style and colour are important.	

Marks

9. A boy describes a sailing trip with his father from America to the Canary Islands.

 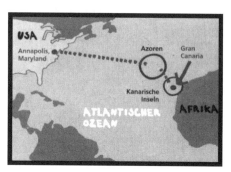

ABENTEUER AUF SEE

Am dritten Tag rief mein Vater plötzlich, „Sieh mal, ein Wal!" Fünfmal insgesamt kam der Wal aus dem Wasser und atmete schwer. „Gut 15 Meter ist er lang," meinte mein Vater. Der Wal schwamm direkt vor unserem Boot.

Das Schlimmste und Schrecklichste auf der Reise war der Sturm. Am Mittwoch, als ich erwachte, war es acht Uhr morgens. Der Wind heulte fürchterlich. Mitte des nächsten Tages ließ der Sturm nach.

(a) One day they saw a whale. What did it do? Write **two** things. **(2)**

_____

_____

(b) What was the whale like? Write **one** thing. **(1)**

_____

(c) When did the storm die down? **(1)**

_____

[*END OF QUESTION PAPER*]

GERMAN
STANDARD GRADE
General Level
Listening Transcript

Transcript—General Level

Instructions to reader(s):

For each item, read the English **once,** then read the German **twice**, with an interval of 7 seconds between the two readings. On completion of the second reading, pause for the length of time indicated in brackets after each item, to allow the candidates to write their answers.

Where special arrangements have been agreed in advance to allow the reading of the material, those sections marked **(f)** should be read by a female speaker and those marked **(m)** by a male: those sections marked **(t)** should be read by the teacher.

(t) You are staying with a German family in Friedrichsstadt, a small town in North Germany.

**(f) or
(m)** **Du wohnst bei einer deutschen Familie in Friedrichsstadt, einer Kleinstadt in Norddeutschland.**

(t) Question number one.

Your pen friend, Jörg, has arranged for you to visit his school.

When do you have to be at school tomorrow?

(m) **Ich habe organisiert, daß du morgen mit mir in die Schule kommst. Wir müssen um Viertel vor acht da sein.**

(30 seconds)

(t) Question number two.

What subject does Jörg have Period 3 tomorrow?

(m) **Ich habe morgen eine Doppelstunde Englisch, und dann in der dritten Stunde Mathe.**

(30 seconds)

(t) Question number three.

Jörg explains how you will get to school.

Tick **three** boxes to show how you will get there.

(m) **Zuerst fahren wir mit dem Rad zum Bahnhof. Dann geht's mit dem Zug weiter. Die Schule ist dann nur fünf Minuten zu Fuß entfernt.**

(30 seconds)

(t) Question number four.

Jörg suggests what you could do in the afternoon.

What does he suggest? Tick **two** boxes.

(m) **Morgen nachmittag habe ich von 14 bis 15.30 Uhr Handball. Wenn du Lust hast, kannst du mitkommen und sehen, wie wir Handball spielen. Oder du könntest dir den Hafen ansehen.**

(30 seconds)

(t) Question number five.

In the morning, Jörg's mother prepares a packed lunch for you.

What does she give you to drink?

(f) **Ich habe euch Brötchen geschmiert. Dazu habe ich Joghurt, einen Apfel und zwei Tüten Orangensaft eingepackt. Vergeßt nicht, alles mitzunehmen!**

(30 seconds)

(t) Question number six.

After you get home from school, Jörg tells you what he must do that evening.

What must he do?

What is he preparing for?

(m) **Heute Abend muß ich für eine Stunde zu meiner Musikgruppe in die Stadthalle. Wir üben für ein Konzert, das wir Weihnachten geben.**

(30 seconds)

(t) Question number seven.

Jörg's mother tells you what her other three children do.

Draw a line from each person to show what they do.

(f) **Jörgs Schwester, Inge, ist in Kiel auf der Uni. Sie studiert Tiermedizin. Sein Bruder, Friedel, ist Apotheker in Hamburg, und die kleine Petra geht noch in die Grundschule.**

(30 seconds)

(t) Question number eight.

Jörg's father tells you about his work.

What does he do?

(m) **Ich bin Ingenieur auf der MS Hamburg. Das ist eine große Fähre, die dreimal in der Woche zwischen Hamburg und England fährt.**

(30 seconds)

(t) Question number nine.

How often does Jörg's father have to work?

(m) **Ich habe jede zweite Woche frei und kann also die Zeit hier zu Hause verbringen. Diese Woche habe ich frei und nächste Woche muß ich wieder arbeiten.**

(30 seconds)

(t) Question number ten.

Jörg's mother suggests what you could all do on Saturday.

What does she suggest doing?

(f) **Mein Mann muß Samstag am frühen Morgen wieder nach Hamburg zum Schiff. Wir könnten alle nach Hamburg fahren. Wir könnten an Bord zu Mittag essen und nachmittags mit der U-Bahn in die Stadtmitte fahren.**

(30 seconds)

(t) Question number eleven.

Jörg suggests what you could do on Saturday night.

What does he suggest? Write **two** things.

(m) **Ja, das ist eine tolle Idee. Wir könnten dann am Samstagabend ins Kino gehen. Nachher könnten wir alle bei meinem Bruder Friedel übernachten.**

(30 seconds)

(t) Question number twelve.

Jörg's mother says she will phone his brother Friedel. You hear the conversation.

What do you hear her say? Tick **two** boxes.

(f) **Hallo Friedel! Morgen kommen wir alle nach Hamburg. Wir werden Samstag Abend gegen 19.00 Uhr bei dir ankommen.**

(30 seconds)

(t) Question number thirteen.

Jörg's mother tells you what Friedel has said on the phone.

What will you do with Friedel on Sunday morning? Write **one** thing.

(f) **Friedel hat euch am Sonntagvormittag zum Schlittschuhlaufen eingeladen. Das Eisstadion ist nicht weit von seiner Wohnung.**

(30 seconds)

(t) Question number fourteen.

What will you do with Friedel in the afternoon? Write **three** things.

(f) **Am Nachmittag macht ihr einen kleinen Sonntagsspaziergang. Friedel will euch ein bißchen von der Stadt zeigen. Gegen vier Uhr gibt's dann Kaffee und Kuchen bei Friedel.**

(30 seconds)

(t) End of test.

You now have 5 minutes to look over your answers.

[END OF TRANSCRIPT]

1999
WEDNESDAY, 26 MAY
11.55 AM – 12.20 PM
(APPROX)

GERMAN
STANDARD GRADE
General Level
Listening

When you are told to do so, open your paper.

You will hear a number of short items in German. You will hear each item twice, then you will have time to write your answer.

Write your answers, **in English**, in this book, in the appropriate spaces.

You may take notes as you are listening to the German, but only in this paper.

You may **not** use a German dictionary.

You are not allowed to leave the examination room until the end of the test.

Before leaving the examination room you must give this book to the invigilator. If you do not, you may lose all the marks for this paper.

Marks

You are staying with a German family in Friedrichsstadt, a small town in North Germany.

Du wohnst bei einer deutschen Familie in Friedrichsstadt, einer Kleinstadt in Norddeutschland.

1. Your pen friend, Jörg, has arranged for you to visit his school.

   When do you have to be at school tomorrow? **(1)**

   _____

   *   *   *   *   *

2. What subject does Jörg have Period 3 tomorrow? **(1)**

   _____

   *   *   *   *   *

3. Jörg explains how you will get to school.

   Tick (✓) **three** boxes to show how you will get there. **(3)**

	Tick (✓)
Bike	
Bus	
Car	
Train	
Tram	
On foot	

   *   *   *   *   *

4. Jörg suggests what you could do in the afternoon.

What does he suggest? Tick (✓) **two** boxes. **(2)**

	Tick (✓)
Watch him playing handball	
Watch handball on TV	
Go on a boat trip	
Visit harbour	
Go shopping	

*   *   *   *   *

5. In the morning, Jörg's mother prepares a packed lunch for you.

What does she give you to drink? **(1)**

_____

*   *   *   *   *

6. After you get home from school, Jörg tells you what he must do that evening.

(*a*) What must he do? **(1)**

_____

(*b*) What is he preparing for? **(1)**

_____

*   *   *   *   *

Marks

7. Jörg's mother tells you what her other three children do.
Draw a line from each person to show what they do. **(3)**

Inge

| bank clerk |

| teacher |

Friedel

| school pupil |

| chemist |

Petra

| doctor |

| student |

*　　*　　*　　*　　*

8. Jörg's father tells you about his work.

What does he do? **(1)**

_____

*　　*　　*　　*　　*

9. How often does Jörg's father have to work? **(1)**

_____

*　　*　　*　　*　　*

10. Jörg's mother suggests what you could all do on Saturday.

What does she suggest doing? **(3)**

Saturday morning	
Saturday lunchtime	
Saturday afternoon	

*　　*　　*　　*　　*

Marks

11. Jörg suggests what you could do on Saturday night.

What does he suggest? Write **two** things. **(2)**

_____

_____

*   *   *   *   *

12. Jörg's mother says she will phone his brother Friedel. You hear the conversation.

What do you hear her say? Tick (✓) **two** boxes. **(2)**

WE'RE ALL COMING TO HAMBURG TOMORROW. ☐

WILL YOU BE IN HAMBURG TOMORROW? ☐

WE WILL ARRIVE ON SATURDAY. ☐

WE WILL ARRIVE ON SUNDAY. ☐

*   *   *   *   *

13. Jörg's mother tells you what Friedel has said on the phone.

What will you do with Friedel on Sunday morning? Write **one** thing. **(1)**

_____

*   *   *   *   *

14. What will you do with Friedel in the afternoon? Write **three** things.

(3)

_____

_____

_____

*   *   *   *   *

[*END OF QUESTION PAPER*]

GERMAN
STANDARD GRADE
General Level
(Optional Paper)
Writing

When you are told to do so, open your paper and write your answers **in German** in the spaces provided.

You may use a German dictionary.

Before leaving the examination room you must give this book to the invigilator. If you do not, you may lose all the marks for this paper.

You are answering a letter from your German pen friend.

Note: Examples are given to help you with ideas. These are only suggestions and you are free to use ideas of your own.

1. You are asked to write a few sentences about your home. You could say, for example, where your home is, whether you live in a house or a flat, the number of bedrooms you have, whether you have a garden, etc. Write at least **three** sentences.

2. You are then asked to write about your morning routine. You could mention, for example, the time you wake up, what you have for breakfast, the time you leave home, when you arrive at school, etc. Write at least **three** sentences.

3. You write about the type of food and drink you enjoy. You could mention, for example, what your favourite meal is and what you like to drink, a café you like to go to, how often you go there, who you go with, etc. Write at least **three** sentences.

4. Your pen friend asks about the clothes you wear. You could mention, for example, what you wear at school, what you wear to a party, where you buy your clothes, etc. Write at least **three** sentences.

5. You are going to Germany next summer. Your pen friend has suggested going to a theme park called Heide-Park. Ask him/her some questions about the visit. You could ask, for example, how you get there, how far it is, what it costs to get in, what you can do there, etc. Ask at least **three** questions.

[END OF QUESTION PAPER]

NATIONAL
QUALIFICATIONS
000

WEDNESDAY, 7 JUNE
G/C 9.20 AM – 10.05 AM
F/G 10.05 AM – 10.50 AM

GERMAN
STANDARD GRADE
General Level
Reading

When you are told to do so, open your paper and write your answers **in English** in the spaces provided.

You may use a German dictionary.

Before leaving the examination room you must give this book to the invigilator. If you do not, you may lose all the marks for this paper.

Marks

Your German pen friend has sent you a magazine to read.

1. A boy writes about his dog.

Mein Hund

Mein Hund ist ein Dackel. Er ist nicht sehr groß und ist sehr intelligent. Am liebsten mag ich ihn, weil er so freundlich ist.

What does he like **best** about his dog? Tick (✓) the correct box.   **1**

	Tick (✓)
It is small.	
It is very clever.	
It is friendly.	

Marks

2. These young people write about holiday jobs they have done.

Ich habe einmal in den Ferien für einen Freund Zeitungen ausgetragen. Für nur drei Stunden die Woche habe ich 50DM verdient. Das war ganz prima.

Sven

Mein bester Ferienjob war als Eisverkäufer am Strand.

Ich bin in der Sonne schön braun geworden.

Daniel

Letztes Jahr habe ich für eine Nachbarfamilie gearbeitet. Ich mußte auf die Kinder aufpassen und mit der Hausarbeit helfen.

Das habe ich aber gern gemacht, weil ich Kinder sehr mag.

Anne

(*a*) What jobs did these young people do?

(*b*) What did they like about their jobs?

6

Sven	Job: _____ Why he liked it: _____ _____
Daniel	Job: _____ Why he liked it: _____ _____
Anne	Job (Write **two** things): _____ _____ Why she liked it: _____ _____

3. This article is about the girl on the front cover of the magazine.

Marks

Ich heiße Anne-Marie, bin sechzehn Jahre alt und komme aus Bremen.

In meiner Freizeit spiele ich Fußball und segle gern mit meinem Freund. Ich lese gern.

Ich hasse Leute, die mit offenem Mund essen.

Complete the grid.

4

Name	Anne-Marie
Age	16
Interests/Hobbies Write three things.	
Dislikes	

4. You see an advert for a zoo. The map shows you how to get there.

Marks

Fahr auf der A5 Richtung Kassel. Du nimmst die zweite Straße links und dann die erste rechts. Nach einem Kilometer fährst du wieder links. Der Zooeingang ist auf der linken Seite.

Mark the zoo on the map. Tick (✓) the correct box.

1

5. You read a long-range weather forecast for the month of August.

Bis zur Mitte des Monats bleibt das sommerliche Wetter mit viel Sonnenschein und hohen Temperaturen wie im Juli.

In der zweiten Hälfte des Monats ändert sich das Wetter. Das Thermometer sinkt um drei bis fünf Grad und am Ende des Monats gibt es ziemlich viel Regen.

What will the weather be like?

4

First half of August? (Write **two** things.)	
Second half of August? (Write **two** things.)	

6. Your uncle is going to have a holiday in Germany. You show him this advert *Marks*
from your magazine.

Hotel
zum
Sänger

Tick (✓)

* Freizeitzentrum und Schwimmbad im Hotel	☐
* Viele Haustiere für unsere Gästekinder	☐
* Saubere und moderne Gästezimmer	☐
* Gutes Restaurant mit Blick auf die Berge	☐
* Nur 800m von der Stadtmitte	☐
* Schöne, ruhige Lage	☐

Your uncle wants a hotel with:

* sports facilities
* good, clean rooms
* quiet location

Tick **three** of the boxes above to show that the hotel has what he is looking
for.

3

7. These young people write about their wishes.

Markus

Die Erwachsenen sollen mir zuhören, wenn ich Probleme habe.

Steffi

Ich wünsche mir, daß alle Kinder ohne Angst vor Bomben leben können.

Elmar

Ich möchte eine bessere Arbeitsstelle finden, weil ich meine Arbeit in der Fabrik stinklangweilig finde.

Inge

Ich möchte, daß die Schule später anfängt und daß wir längere Ferien haben.

What do they wish? Write **one** thing for each person.   **4**

Markus _____

_____

Steffi _____

_____

Elmar _____

_____

Inge _____

_____

8. You see an advert for a special kind of T-shirt.

In der Stadtmitte siehst du einen Jungen. Du möchtest ihn kennenlernen. Aber wie?

Zum Glück trägt er ein 'E-shirt.' Da steht seine E-mail Adresse gleich hinten drauf, und du kannst ihn einfach anmailen. Das E-shirt bekommst du für 39,90 Mark über die Web-site www.adresse.de.

Complete these sentences:

(*a*) The T-shirt is special because it has _____   **1**

_____ on it.

(*b*) You can buy it for 39.90 Marks from _____   **1**

_____.

9. This article is about how to help the environment.

1. Kochst du Wasser, dann leg immer einen Deckel auf den Topf. Das Wasser kocht schneller und du sparst Energie.

2. Energiesparen in deinem Zimmer: laß nie eine Lampe brennen. Dreh die Heizung zurück, ein Pullover wärmt auch!

3. Achte darauf, daß auch in deiner Familie Müll getrennt wird. Bring selbst jede Woche das Altglas zum Container.

4. Geh zu Fuß oder nimm das Fahrrad, wenn du kurze Strecken hast. Nur im Notfall bitte die Eltern, dich mit dem Auto hinzufahren.

Match the words with the pictures. Write the correct number in each box. **3**

Picture	Number
A	
B	
C	
D	

10. This article gives you some tips about how to be happy.

Super-Happy!

5 Tips für gute Laune!

A. Neue Pläne sind ein guter Weg aus einem Tief. Schreib 10 Sachen auf, die du machen willst!

B. Neue Klamotten und eine andere Frisur wirken Wunder.

C. Wenn du gut und viel schläfst, fühlst du dich viel besser.

D. Setz dich ruhig in eine Ecke und lies mal ein gutes Buch oder hör dir eine CD an!

E. Mit dem Rad statt mit dem Bus zur Schule fahren.

Match the tips to the headings below. Write the correct letter in each box.

4

	Letter
Keep fit.	
Get enough sleep.	
Make resolutions.	
Do some reading and relaxing.	
Change your appearance.	

Total (32)

[END OF QUESTION PAPER]

NATIONAL
QUALIFICATIONS
2000

WEDNESDAY, 7 JUNE
11.55 AM – 12.20 PM
(APPROX)

GERMAN
STANDARD GRADE
General Level
Listening Transcript

Transcript—General Level

Instructions to reader(s):

For each item, read the English **once,** then read the German **three times,** with an interval of 5 seconds between the readings. On completion of the third reading, pause for the length of time indicated in brackets after each item, to allow the candidates to write their answers.

Where special arrangements have been agreed in advance to allow the reading of the material, those sections marked **(f)** should be read by a female speaker and those marked **(m)** by a male: those sections marked **(t)** should be read by the teacher.

(t) You are youth hostelling in Germany.

**(f) or
(m)** **Du bist auf Urlaub in Deutschland. Du übernachtest in Jugendherbergen.**

(t) Question number one.

You arrive at a hostel. The warden speaks to you.

Do you get a single room? When is breakfast? Tick the correct boxes.

**(f) or
(m)** **Guten Tag! Also, du hast ein Zimmer zusammen mit drei anderen. Es gibt um halb acht Frühstück.**

(30 seconds)

(t) Question number two.

You get to know a boy called Dieter. He invites you to join him for the day.

What does he want to do in town? Tick **two** boxes.

(m) **Hast du Lust, mit in die Stadt zu gehen? Zuerst muß ich zur Post - ich brauche Briefmarken. Ich gehe später ins Automobilmuseum. Dort gibt es tolle Autos.**

(30 seconds)

(t) Question number three.

You are in town with Dieter. You go to a restaurant for lunch.

What does Dieter order? Tick the **three** correct items on the menu.

(m) **Das Essen hier ist immer sehr gut. Ich glaube, ich nehme die Tomatensuppe und . . . das Hähnchen mit Salzkartoffeln. Als Nachtisch nehme ich den Eisbecher!**

(30 seconds)

(t) Question number four.

In the restaurant, Dieter shows you a picture of his family.

Which of these people is his younger sister? Put a tick at the correct person.

(m) **Das ist meine Familie. Die hier rechts ist meine ältere Schwester, Monika. Das hier ist meine Kusine, Barbara. Ganz links ist meine jüngere Schwester, Christine.**

(30 seconds)

(t) Question number five.

Dieter asks you about where you live.

What does he want to know? Tick **two** things.

(m) **Wie groß ist deine Stadt? Ich meine, wie viele leben dort? Wohnst du in einem Haus mit Garten oder in einer Wohnung?**

(30 seconds)

(t) Question number six.

Dieter invites you to go on a coach trip the next day to see something of the area.

Where does the trip leave from?

(m) **Also, morgen machen wir einen Ausflug mit dem Bus. Abfahrt ist am Marktplatz.**

(30 seconds)

(t) Question number seven.

He explains what you will do on the trip.

What will you do in the morning and in the afternoon?

(m) **Am Morgen besuchen wir ein herrliches altes Schloß. Da hat unser König Ludwig gelebt. Am Nachmittag machen wir eine Bootsfahrt auf dem See.**

(30 seconds)

(t) Question number eight.

At the youth hostel, you meet a girl called Sandra. She says she will be playing at a concert tomorrow in the town hall.

What else does she tell you about herself? Write **two** things.

(f) **Ich komme aus Bern in der Schweiz. Ich bin mit meinem Schulorchester hier. Morgen geben wir ein Konzert. Ich spiele Klavier.**

(30 seconds)

(t) Question number nine.

Sandra gives you a ticket for the concert. She tells you how to get there.

How can you get there? Tick **two** of the boxes.

(f) **Du fährst mit der Straßenbahn, Linie 8, bis zum Stadion. Oder du kannst auch zu Fuß hingehen, wenn du Lust hast.**

(30 seconds)

(t) Question number ten.

She gives you directions from the stadium to the hall where they are playing.

Put a cross on the plan to show where the hall is.

(f) **Vom Stadion gehst du geradeaus. Du nimmst die zweite Straße links. Die Halle findest du dann auf der rechten Seite.**

(30 seconds)

(t) Question number eleven.

You hear Sandra telling a friend on the phone what she likes and doesn't like about her stay at the youth hostel.

What does she **not** like? Tick **two** boxes.

(f) **Die Leute hier sind sehr freundlich, muß ich sagen. Mein Zimmer . . . mag ich nicht so sehr: Es ist ziemlich klein . . . Das Essen hier schmeckt wirklich gut. Das Wetter? Du liebe Zeit! Scheußlich, es regnet jeden Tag!**

(30 seconds)

(t) Question number twelve.

Sandra invites you to her parents' flat for a few days.

What does she tell you about their flat? Write **two** things.

(f) **Wir haben eine Fünfzimmerwohnung. Sie liegt in der Stadtmitte. Wir haben Platz genug für dich.**

(30 seconds)

(t) Question number thirteen.

She says you could also visit her grandparents.

What does she say about where they live? Write **two** things.

(f) **Wir könnten auch meine Großeltern besuchen. Sie wohnen in einem kleinen Dorf in den Bergen, 50 Kilometer von Bern entfernt.**

(30 seconds)

(t) Question number fourteen.

How will you get to Sandra's flat?

How long will it take to get there?

(f) **Mein Vater kommt am Wochenende mit dem Auto. Wir können zusammen mit ihm nach Hause fahren. Die Reise dauert ungefähr zwei Stunden.**

(30 seconds)

(t) End of test.

Now look over your answers.

[END OF TRANSCRIPT]

NATIONAL
QUALIFICATIONS
2000

WEDNESDAY, 7 JUNE
11.55 AM – 12.20 PM
(APPROX)

GERMAN
STANDARD GRADE
General Level
Listening

When you are told to do so, open your paper.

You will hear a number of short items in German. You will hear each item three times, then you will have time to write your answer.

Write your answers, **in English**, in this book, in the appropriate spaces.

You may take notes as you are listening to the German, but only in this paper.

You may **not** use a German dictionary.

You are not allowed to leave the examination room until the end of the test.

Before leaving the examination room you must give this book to the invigilator. If you do not, you may lose all the marks for this paper.

Marks

You are youth hostelling in Germany.

Du bist auf Urlaub in Deutschland. Du übernachtest in Jugendherbergen.

1. You arrive at a hostel. The warden speaks to you. Tick (✓) the correct boxes.　　2

(*a*)　Do you get a single room?　　Yes ☐　　No ☐

(*b*)　When is breakfast?　　7.30 ☐　　8.30 ☐

*　　*　　*　　*　　*

2. You get to know a boy called Dieter. He invites you to join him for the day.

What does he want to do in town? Tick (✓) **two** boxes.　　2

	Tick (✓)
Buy postcards	
Buy stamps	
Go to a museum	
Hire a car	

*　　*　　*　　*　　*

71

Marks

3. You are in town with Dieter. You go to a restaurant for lunch.

What does Dieter order? Tick (✓) the **three** correct items on the menu.

3

Mushroom soup	☐
Tomato soup	☐
Pea soup	☐

Chicken	☐
Ham	☐
Pork	☐

Apple tart	☐
Fruit salad	☐
Ice cream	☐

*   *   *   *   *

4. In the restaurant, Dieter shows you a picture of his family.

Which of these people is his younger sister? Put a tick (✓) at the correct person.

1

*   *   *   *   *

Marks

5. Dieter asks you about where you live.

What does he want to know? Tick (✓) **two** things.   **2**

He wants to know . . .

	Tick (✓)
. . . where your town is.	
. . . how many people live there.	
. . . how long you have stayed there.	
. . . the kind of house you live in.	

*   *   *   *   *

6. Dieter invites you to go on a coach trip the next day to see something of the area.

Where does the trip leave from?   **1**

_____

*   *   *   *   *

7. He explains what you will do on the trip. What will you do:

(*a*)   In the morning? _____   **1**

(*b*)   In the afternoon? _____   **1**

*   *   *   *   *

8. At the youth hostel, you meet a girl called Sandra. She says she will be playing at a concert tomorrow in the town hall.

What else does she tell you about herself? Write **two** things.   **2**

_____

_____

*   *   *   *   *

Marks

9. Sandra gives you a ticket for the concert. She tells you how to get there.

How can you get there?   Tick (✓) **two** of the boxes.   **2**

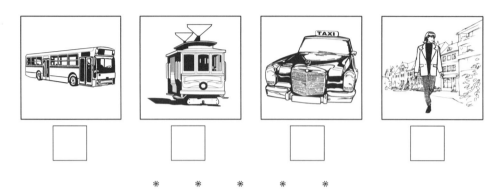

*　　*　　*　　*　　*

10. She gives you directions from the stadium to the hall where they are playing.

Put a cross (✗) on the plan to show where the hall is.   **1**

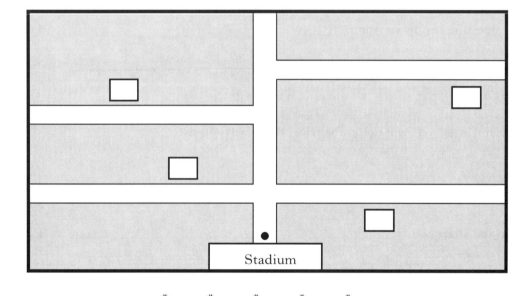

*　　*　　*　　*　　*

Marks

11. You hear Sandra telling a friend on the phone what she likes and doesn't like about her stay at the youth hostel.

What does she **not** like? Tick (✓) **two** boxes.   2

	Tick (✓)
The people	
Her room	
The food	
The weather	

*   *   *   *   *

12. Sandra invites you to her parents' flat for a few days.

What does she tell you about their flat? Write **two** things.   2

_____

_____

*   *   *   *   *

13. She says you could also visit her grandparents.

What does she say about where they live? Write **two** things.   2

_____

_____

*   *   *   *   *

14. (*a*) How will you get to Sandra's flat?   1

_____

(*b*) How long will it take to get there?   1

_____

*   *   *   *   *

Total (26)

[*END OF QUESTION PAPER*]

NATIONAL
QUALIFICATIONS
2000

MONDAY, 12 JUNE
1.30 PM – 2.15 PM

GERMAN
STANDARD GRADE
General Level
(Additional)
Writing

When you are told to do so, open your paper and write your answers **in German** in the spaces provided.

You may use a German dictionary.

Before leaving the examination room you must give this book to the invigilator. If you do not, you may lose all the marks for this paper.

You are writing an e-mail to your German pen friend.

Note: Examples are given to help you with ideas. These are only suggestions and you are free to use ideas of your own.

1. Your pen friend wants to know what you do at the week-end. You could mention, for example, when you get up, whether you work at the week-end, what you do on Sundays, etc. Write at least **three** sentences.

2. You have found an American pen friend via the Internet. Tell your German pen friend about this person. You could mention, for example, how old he/she is, where he/she lives, what he/she does in his/her spare time, etc. Write at least **three** sentences.

3. You are planning to go to a concert.

   You could tell your pen friend where and when the concert is, how you plan to get there, who you are going with, etc. Write at least **three** sentences.

4. You want to find out more about your pen friend's school. You could ask, for example, how he/she gets to school, when school starts/finishes, what subjects he/she likes, etc. Ask at least **three** questions.

5. Your school is running a Healthy Living Week. Tell your pen friend what you are doing to get fit.

You could mention, for example, what sport you do and how often, what you eat and drink, when you go to bed, etc. Write at least **three** sentences.

[END OF QUESTION PAPER]

1997
WEDNESDAY, 28 MAY
1.45 PM – 2.45 PM

GERMAN
STANDARD GRADE
Credit Level
Reading

Instructions to the Candidate

When you are told to do so, open your paper and write your answers **in English** in the **separate** answer book provided.

You may use a German dictionary.

Your German pen friend has sent you a magazine to read.   *Marks*

1. Alexander is a boy from Berlin who is physically disabled. He writes about some of the unpleasant things that sometimes happen to him on the way to school.

> Ich fahre mit der U-Bahn zur Schule. Ich gehe den Weg zur U-Bahnstation meistens allein, weil meine Mitschüler so schnell laufen, daß ich nicht mithalten kann. Auf dem Bahnsteig steht eine Mutter mit ihrer kleinen Tochter. „Guck mal, Mami! Warum läuft der da so komisch?" fragt das Mädchen.
>
> Beim Aussteigen werde ich geschoben und gestoßen. „Nicht so langsam, andere wollen auch noch aussteigen", ruft jemand.

(a) What unpleasant things happen to Alexander on the way to school? Write **three** things.   **(3)**

The last part of his journey is by bus. He describes an occasion when he sat on the seat reserved for disabled people.

> Vom Bahnhof muß ich noch ein paar Stationen mit dem Bus fahren. Ich habe Glück und finde Platz auf der Bank vorne beim Fahrer, die für Behinderte reserviert ist. Eine ältere Frau steigt ein und kommt direkt auf meinen Platz zu. Sie sagt: „Geh mal weg da! Du siehst doch, daß ich mich setzen will."
>
> „Das ist ein Platz für Schwerbeschädigte", sagt mir eine zweite Frau. „Steh auf, und laß die Dame sitzen!"
>
> Dann sagt der Busfahrer: „So etwas Unverschämtes habe ich schon lange nicht mehr gesehen! Kannst du denn nicht lesen?" Nun habe ich aber genug. Ich halte meinen Ausweis hoch und rufe laut: „Das hier ist mein Behindertenausweis. Ich darf hier sitzen." Auf einmal wird es ganz still im Bus.

(b) What did the following people say to him?

   (i)   the elderly woman

   (ii) the second woman

   (iii) the bus driver   **(3)**

(c) How did Alexander deal with the situation? Write **two** things.   **(2)**

2. This article is about the kind of role models young people have.

Hast du ein Vorbild?

Für viele junge Leute ist der Lieblingssportler ein Vorbild, für andere der Lieblingssänger.

Aber für uns alle waren unsere Eltern die ersten Vorbilder. Wie man läuft oder wie man spricht, das alles lernen wir von den Eltern!

Wenn wir größer werden, kommen andere Vorbilder an die Stelle der Eltern. Diese Vorbilder suchen wir uns nach Eigenschaften aus, die wir selbst gern hätten: Gutes Aussehen, Kraft, Erfolg, Geduld.

(*a*) Parents are our first role models. What do we learn from them? Write **two** things. **(2)**

(*b*) How do we choose our role models when we are older? **(2)**

Für einen Star oder ein Idol zu schwärmen ist nichts Schlimmes. Man muß sich nur klarmachen, daß auch berühmte Leute Fehler haben wie du und ich!
Aber Vorbilder müssen ja nicht immer Stars und reich sein. Es gibt auch Menschen, die Vorbilder sind—weil sie nicht an sich sondern an andere denken. Wie zum Beispiel die Leute, die in Afrika arbeiten und dort den armen Menschen helfen.

(*c*) What must we remember about the famous people we have as role models? **(1)**

(*d*) Why might aid workers in Africa be good role models? **(1)**

Marks

3. Three young people describe how they would try to get into conversation with someone they see in a café.

Franci

Es ist altmodisch, aber ich erwarte, daß die Jungen auf mich zugehen. Wenn mich jemand besonders interessiert, dann finde ich, man soll nicht einfach passiv da sitzen.

Ich stelle mich zum Beispiel im Café so hin, daß der Junge in meine Richtung gucken muß!

Das Wichtigste ist, daß der Junge mich anspricht und nicht umgekehrt.

Uwe

Wenn mir ein Mädchen im Café gefällt, dann setze ich mich einfach neben sie. Meistens überlege ich mir schon vorher, was ich sagen soll.

Zum Beispiel: „Ich weiß nicht, was ich bestellen soll, mach mir bitte einen Vorschlag." Viele lachen dann, und wir können weitersprechen!

Daniela

Ich versuche es erst mal mit Blickkontakt. In dem Moment, wo der Junge zufällig herschaut, gucke ich ihm in die Augen und dann sofort wieder weg. Dann versuche ich, mit ihm ins Gespräch zu kommen.

Franci, Uwe and Daniela all take different approaches when getting into conversation with someone.

(*a*) What approach does Franci take? Write **two** things. (2)

(*b*) What approach does Uwe take? Write **two** things. (2)

(*c*) What approach does Daniela take? Write **two** things. (2)

Marks

4. The writer of this article is a girl called Yvonne. She asks what would happen if pupils gave **teachers** grades, instead of the other way round.

- **Dann könnten die Kinder, wenn ein Lehrer etwas schlecht erklärt, sagen: „Das war ganz schlecht! Bis nächsten Montag bereiten Sie das besser vor!"**
- **. . . und die Kinder könnten zum Lehrer sagen: „Nehmen Sie sich ein Beispiel am Lehrer der Klasse 3d. Der ist ein guter Lehrer."**
- **. . . und dann hätten viele Lehrer vor der Schule genausoviel Angst wie viele Schüler.**

(*a*) What does Yvonne think would happen if pupils were to give teachers grades? Write **three** things. **(3)**

Viele Lehrer würden Hilfe brauchen, um bessere Lehrer zu werden. Und wer könnte einem Lehrer helfen? Natürlich ein Kind!

Und weil ich weiß, wie ein guter Lehrer sein sollte, könnte ich mir dann mit Nachhilfestunden mein Taschengeld aufbessern. Und bei dem, was wir in der Schule an Lehrern so haben, könnte ich auch noch meiner Mutter einen neuen Wintermantel kaufen.

(*b*) Yvonne thinks teachers would need help in order to become better teachers. Why does she feel qualified to help them improve? **(1)**

(*c*) How will she and her mother benefit? **(2)**

Total (26)

[END OF QUESTION PAPER]

GERMAN
STANDARD GRADE
Credit Level
Listening Transcript

Transcript—Credit Level

Instructions to reader(s):

For each item, read the English **once,** then read the German **twice**, with an interval of 7 seconds between the two readings. On completion of the second reading, pause for the length of time indicated in brackets after each item, to allow the candidates to write their answers.

Where special arrangements have been agreed in advance to allow the reading of the material, those sections marked **(f)** should be read by a female speaker and those marked **(m)** by a male: those sections marked **(t)** should be read by the teacher.

(t) You are staying with your pen friend, Peter, in Germany.

Question number one.

One evening you are about to go to a party.

What advice does Peter's mother give you? Write **three** things.

(f)   **Wenn die Party erst nach Mitternacht zu Ende ist, lauft nicht allein nach Hause! Es ist zu gefährlich. Es ist schon viel passiert. Wenn ihr genug Leute findet, teilt euch ein Taxi! Oder übernachtet bei eurem Freund!**

(40 seconds)

(t) Question number two.

At the party, you are introduced to some of Peter's friends.

What questions do they ask you? Write **three** things.

(f) or (m)   **—Ich habe dich heute in der Schule gesehen, nicht wahr? Wie gefällt es dir in unserer Schule?**

(f) or (m)   **—Ist Deutsch deine erste Fremdsprache?**

(f) or (m)   **—Welche Sprache ist beliebter in Schottland—Deutsch oder Französisch?**

(40 seconds)

(t) Question number three.

One of Peter's friends is Ali, a boy from a Turkish family.

Why does Ali feel his family may one day go back to Turkey? Write **two** things.

(m)   1965, als mein Vater nach Deutschland kam, gab es viele Arbeitsplätze. Junge Leute finden es heutzutage schwer, eine Stelle zu bekommen. Wenn ich keine Stelle oder keinen Studienplatz kriege, dann werden wir bestimmt in die Türkei zurückkehren. Und außerdem denke ich, daß meine Eltern Heimweh nach der Türkei haben und irgendwann zurückgehen wollen.

(40 seconds)

(t) Question number four.

Ali tells you about how his father travelled to Germany when he first came from Turkey.

What does he say about the journey? Write **two** things.

(m)   Die Familie meines Vaters wohnte auf dem Lande, und seine Reise hat mit einem Pferd angefangen. Vier Stunden mußte er reiten, bis zum Hauptbahnhof. Stellt euch das mal vor! Dann verbrachte er 36 Stunden im Zug.

(40 seconds)

(t) Question number five.

Ali describes his father's first impressions of Germany.

What differences did he notice compared with his old life in Turkey? Write **two** things.

(m)   Als er in Deutschland ankam, fand er das Leben völlig anders als in der Türkei. Die Leute hatten weniger Zeit—alles mußte immer sehr schnell gehen. Außerdem war er sehr einsam. Er vermißte seine Verwandten und Freunde.

(40 seconds)

(t) Question number six.

Things slowly improved for Ali's father after his first two years in Germany.

In what ways did things improve? Write **two** things.

(m)   Als die Familie nach zwei Jahren auch nach Deutschland kommen konnte, war er glücklicher, weil er wieder mit ihnen zusammen sein konnte. Und als wir Kinder, meine Geschwister und ich, in die Schule gingen, lernte er auch mehr Deutsche kennen.

(40 seconds)

(t) Question number seven.

Two girls at the party, Susanne and Karoline, have different views about immigrants.

What does Susanne think immigrants could do to help themselves, and why?

(f)   Ich habe nichts gegen Ausländer, aber sie sollten sich mehr anpassen. Kein Wunder, daß sie sich nicht integrieren können. Ihre Kultur und unsere Kultur passen nicht zusammen. Wenn sie freiwillig hierher kommen, müssen sie sich auch etwas bemühen.

(40 seconds)

(t) Question number eight.

Karoline is more sympathetic towards immigrants.

What is her opinion? Write **two** things.

(f)   Aber viele Leute haben nur Angst vor dem Unbekannten. Ich finde, die Ausländer sollten ihre Kultur nicht aufgeben. Ich möchte jedenfalls keine türkischen, italienischen und griechischen Restaurants missen!

(40 seconds)

(t) Question number nine.

Later that evening, Peter tells you about an appointment he has with the doctor the following day.

What are the reasons for the appointment? Write **two** things.

(m)   Du, am Donnerstag habe ich einen Termin bei meinem Arzt. Im Winter habe ich einen Skiunfall gehabt und habe mir das rechte Bein gebrochen. Zweimal im Jahr muß er kontrollieren, daß alles noch in Ordnung ist.

(40 seconds)

(t) Question number ten.

Peter suggests what you could do while he is at the doctor's.

What does he suggest? Write **two** things.

(m)   Während ich da bin, könntest du vielleicht den Dom besuchen und auf den Turm klettern. Von dort oben hat man einen wunderschönen Blick über die ganze Stadt.

(40 seconds)

(t) Question number eleven.

Peter suggests what you could do together after that.

What does he suggest? Write **three** things.

(m)   Zu Mittag können wir in einem Schnellimbiß essen gehen und dann eventuell auf dem See Kanu fahren. Und ich habe von einem Freund gehört, daß es im Stadtmuseum gerade eine Ausstellung übers Kino gibt. Sie läuft noch bis nächste Woche. Wenn du Lust hast, können wir auch dahin gehen.

(40 seconds)

(t) End of test.

You now have 5 minutes to look over your answers.

[END OF TRANSCRIPT]

GERMAN
STANDARD GRADE
Credit Level
Listening

Instructions to the Candidate

When you are told to do so, open your paper.

You will hear a number of short items in German. You will hear each item twice, then you will have time to write your answer.

Write your answers, **in English**, in the **separate** answer book provided.

You may take notes as you are listening to the German, but only in your answer book.

You may **not** use a German dictionary.

You are not allowed to leave the examination room until the end of the test.

Marks

You are staying with your pen friend, Peter, in Germany.

1. One evening you are about to go to a party.
   What advice does Peter's mother give you? Write **three** things. **(3)**

   *   *   *   *   *

2. At the party, you are introduced to some of Peter's friends.
   What questions do they ask you? Write **three** things. **(3)**

   *   *   *   *   *

3. One of Peter's friends is Ali, a boy from a Turkish family.
   Why does Ali feel his family may one day go back to Turkey? Write **two** things. **(2)**

   *   *   *   *   *

4. Ali tells you about how his father travelled to Germany when he first came from Turkey.
   What does he say about the journey? Write **two** things. **(2)**

   *   *   *   *   *

Marks

5. Ali describes his father's first impressions of Germany.

   What differences did he notice compared with his old life in Turkey? Write **two** things.

   (2)

   *　　*　　*　　*　　*

6. Things slowly improved for Ali's father after his first two years in Germany.

   In what ways did things improve? Write **two** things.

   (2)

   *　　*　　*　　*　　*

7. Two girls at the party, Susanne and Karoline, have different views about immigrants.

   What does Susanne think immigrants could do to help themselves, and why?

   (2)

   *　　*　　*　　*　　*

8. Karoline is more sympathetic towards immigrants.

   What is her opinion? Write **two** things.

   (2)

   *　　*　　*　　*　　*

9. Later that evening, Peter tells you about an appointment he has with the doctor the following day.

   What are the reasons for the appointment? Write **two** things.

   (2)

   *　　*　　*　　*　　*

10. Peter suggests what you could do while he is at the doctor's.

    What does he suggest? Write **two** things.

    (2)

    *　　*　　*　　*　　*

11. Peter suggests what you could do together after that.

    What does he suggest? Write **three** things.

    (3)

    *　　*　　*　　*　　*

    Total (25)

[END OF QUESTION PAPER]

1997
FRIDAY, 30 MAY
10.35 AM – 11.35 AM

GERMAN
STANDARD GRADE
Credit Level
(Optional Paper)
Writing

These young people were asked to write about their life at school and their plans for the future.

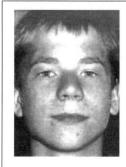

Stefan

Schule finde ich furchtbar. Wir haben immer so viele Hausaufgaben. Ich helfe viel lieber meinem Vater auf dem Bauernhof. Ich möchte auch später Landwirt werden wie mein Vater. Ich glaube, ich gehe in der zehnten Klasse ab.

Claudia

Ich gehe gern zur Schule. Meine Lieblingsfächer sind Französisch und Deutsch. Nach meinem Abitur möchte ich für ein Jahr nach Frankreich gehen und dort arbeiten. Ich möchte meine Sprachkenntnisse verbessern, weil ich gern Fremdsprachensekretärin werden will.

Markus

Mein Lieblingsfach in der Schule ist Musik. Ich spiele Flöte. Während meines Arbeitspraktikums habe ich in einem Musikgeschäft gearbeitet. Ich denke, ich werde später auch ein Geschäft haben und Flöten bauen.

Anna

Ich gehe nicht so gerne in die Schule, aber ich mache gern Sport und Kunst. In Kunst habe ich einen sehr netten Lehrer, der den Unterricht sehr interessant macht. Ich habe vor, die Schule vor dem Abitur zu verlassen, weil ich eine Lehre als Tischler machen möchte. Dafür braucht man kein Abitur.

What are your thoughts on your life at school?

Here are some ideas you may wish to consider. You do not have to use all of them, and you are free to include other relevant ideas.

* What subjects do you like at school?
* What don't you like so much about school?
* How do you get on with your teachers?
* Have you done any work experience?
* Have you any plans for further study?
* What sort of job would you like to do eventually?

Write about 200 words **in German**. You may use a German dictionary.

[END OF QUESTION PAPER]

1998
TUESDAY, 26 MAY
10.15 AM – 11.15 AM

GERMAN
STANDARD GRADE
Credit Level
Reading

Instructions to the Candidate

When you are told to do so, open your paper and write your answers **in English** in the **separate** answer book provided.

You may use a German dictionary.

Your pen friend has sent you a German magazine to read.   *Marks*

1. Three young Germans write about their experiences at English Language summer schools.

Wie war's?
Did you like
it?

„Ich war in Elgin. Japaner, Franzosen, Spanier—auf der Sommerschule in Elgin (Morayshire) in Schottland waren viele Nationen vertreten. Wir hatten jeden Tag zwei Stunden Schule und konnten danach Sportarten wie Kanufahren oder Fechten ausprobieren. Ungewohnt waren für mich die strengen Regeln: Die Mädchen durften sich zum Beispiel nicht mit Jungen treffen. Natürlich sind wir trotzdem nachts aus dem Fenster geklettert und haben zusammen Partys gefeiert."

Birgit

(*a*)   How was the day at Birgit's summer school divided up?   **(1)**

(*b*)   Which school rule did she find surprising?   **(1)**

(*c*)   How did the young people overcome this problem?   **(1)**

Marks

„Ich war in Torquay. Torquay ist ein ganz kleiner englischer Küstenort, der jedes Jahr von Sprachgruppen überschwemmt wird. Die Einheimischen schienen von uns Sprachschülern etwas genervt, so daß es schwer war, mit Gleichaltrigen in Kontakt zu kommen. Aber meine nette Gastfamilie behandelte mich wie ihren eigenen Sohn. Wir haben viel gemeinsam unternommen.“

(*d*)   What did Sven find difficult about his time in Torquay?   **(1)**

(*e*)   What did he enjoy about his visit?   **(1)**

„Ich war in Chicago. Meinen Amerika-Aufenthalt hatte ich mir etwas anders vorgestellt. Meine erste Gastfamilie in Chicago war ein echter Schocker. In der Wohnung sah es aus, als hätte eine Bombe eingeschlagen. Dazu mußte ich mit den zwei kleinen Kindern ein Zimmer teilen. Zum Glück konnte ich nach einer Woche in eine andere Familie wechseln. Der Sprachunterricht zusammen mit Schülern aus aller Welt machte wirklich Spaß.“

(*f*)   Why were things difficult at first for Christoph? (Write **two** things.)   **(2)**

(*g*)   What did he particularly like about the course?   **(1)**

Marks

2. This article is about a woman who does what was once considered a man's job and a man who does what used to be considered a woman's job.

Typisch Frau,

Stephanie Kuhn

← Lokomotiv-führerin

Wenn Stephanie Kuhn als Kind mit ihrer Mutter an einem Bahnübergang stand und eine Diesellokomotive vorbeibrauste, dann sagte sie, „So eine möchte ich auch mal fahren!" Später wurde sie Lokomotivführerin.

Wer eine moderne Diesellokomotive fahren will, muß sich gut konzentrieren können. Stephanie muß natürlich die Fahrpläne genau wissen. Sie darf nicht zu schnell und nicht zu langsam fahren, muß die Signale beachten. Als Lokomotivführerin trägt sie die volle Verantwortung.

„Ich mag die Arbeit sehr, aber der Schichtdienst macht manchmal Probleme. Mein Mann ist ebenfalls Lokomotivführer, und wir müssen also unsere Arbeitszeiten abstimmen, damit einer von uns jeden Abend zu Hause ist und für die Kinder sorgt."

(*a*) What first made Stephanie decide to become an engine driver? **(1)**

(*b*) What is required to be a good engine driver? Write **three** things. **(3)**

(*c*) How does she get round the problem of coping with her children and doing shift work?

(1)

typisch Mann?

Jens Unger is a male midwife. (A midwife is a nurse who specialises in the delivery of babies.)

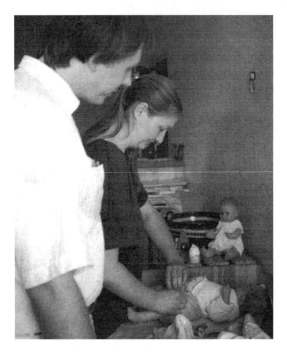

„Für diesen Beruf habe ich mich erst vor wenigen Jahren entschieden", erzählt Jens. „Damals habe ich im Krankenhaus gearbeitet und durfte bei einer Geburt dabei sein. Die Geburt dauerte viele Stunden. Es war sehr schön, zu sehen, wie glücklich und dankbar die Frau war, als ihr Kind endlich da war! Darum wollte ich Entbindungspfleger werden."

Als Entbindungspfleger muß Jens jede Menge über Medizin wissen. „Meine Aufgabe ist es aber auch, die Blicke und Bewegungen der schwangeren Frau richtig zu verstehen. Ich muß auch erkennen, wann es für die Frau und das Baby gefährlich wird."

(*d*) What made Jens decide he wanted to become a midwife? (Write **two** things.) **(2)**

(*e*) What is required to be a good midwife? (Write **three** things.) **(3)**

Marks

3. Two young people tell us what the word "**beauty**" means to them. Each of them had experiences when they were young which affected how they later thought about the subject of beauty.

Was heißt hier „schön“?

Thomas, 17

Wie jemand aussieht, ist für mich nicht so wichtig. Das beeindruckt mich gar nicht.

Als ich zehn Jahre war, habe ich mir das Gesicht schwer verbrannt. In vier Operationen wurde mir mein Gesicht einigermaßen wiederhergestellt. Am Anfang war es schwer, denn ich wurde oft auf der Straße angestarrt, besonders von jungen Leuten. Später jedoch habe ich es ignoriert, und ich bin dadurch selbstbewußter geworden.

Ich habe gelernt, das Äußere nicht mehr so wichtig zu nehmen, und meine Einstellung zu „was ist schön?“ hat sich dadurch geändert. Was für mich jetzt wichtig ist, sind die Charaktereigenschaften: „Schön“ ist, wenn jemand gut mit anderen Leuten umgehen kann und Toleranz zeigt.

Anja, 16

Das typische Schönheitsideal hat mich eine Zeitlang kaputtgemacht. Mit zehn Jahren war ich dick, trug eine Brille und wurde von meinen Klassenkameraden ständig ausgelacht. In den Zeitschriften sah ich die dünnen Models und ich habe mir eingeredet: so mußt du aussehen! Ich habe alles getan, um abzunehmen. Keinen Zucker mehr essen und Sport treiben. Ich habe so viel abgenommen, daß ich krank geworden bin. Ich lag wochenlang im Krankenhaus und habe ein Schuljahr wiederholen müssen.

Heute fühle ich mich wohl, so wie ich bin, und mache mir keine Gedanken mehr ums Aussehen. „Schön“ bedeutet für mich deshalb, das Leben positiv zu betrachten und innerlich zufrieden zu sein.

(a) What were the experiences which affected how they later thought about beauty? Write **two** things for each person.   **(4)**

(b) What does "beauty" mean for them now? Write **two** things for each person.   **(4)**

Total (26)

[END OF QUESTION PAPER]

1998
TUESDAY, 26 MAY
1.00 PM – 1.30 PM
(APPROX)

GERMAN
STANDARD GRADE
Credit Level
Listening Transcript

Transcript—Credit Level

Instructions to reader(s):

For each item, read the English **once**, then read the German **twice**, with an interval of 7 seconds between the two readings. On completion of the second reading, pause for the length of time indicated in brackets after each item, to allow the candidates to write their answers.

Where special arrangements have been agreed in advance to allow the reading of the material, those sections marked **(f)** should be read by a female speaker and those marked **(m)** by a male: those sections marked **(t)** should be read by the teacher.

(t) During the summer you spend two weeks at an international summer school for young people in Munich.

**(f) or
(m)** **Während des Sommers besuchst du zwei Wochen lang eine internationale Sommerschule für Jugendliche in München.**

(t) Question number one.

When you arrive, you meet two fellow students.

How did they travel to the summer school? Write **two** things.

**(f) or
(m)** **Hallo! Wir sind gerade angekommen. Wir sind beide aus Finnland und haben uns auf der Fähre getroffen. Die Überfahrt haben wir am Freitag gemacht, und dann sind wir gemeinsam mit dem Zug von Kiel hierhergereist. Woher kommst du?**

(40 seconds)

(t) Question number two.

You all go to the reception desk, where you are given some information.

What information are you given? Write **three** things.

**(f) or
(m)** **Ihr habt euch schon eingetragen? Ja? Gut. Also, ihr drei seid im Zimmer 24. Das liegt im zweiten Stock. Schlafsäcke und Handtücher findet ihr auf den Betten. Ich wünsche euch allen viel Spaß.**

(40 seconds)

(t) Question number three.

You are told to come to the hall at 11.00 am. The group leader tells you about arrangements for meals and snacks.

What does she tell you? Write **three** things.

(f) **Es gibt drei Mahlzeiten pro Tag. Die Zeiten findet ihr am Brett vor dem Speisesaal. Vegetarier sollten sich heute bei der Küche melden. Am Kiosk kann man außerdem noch Süßigkeiten und Getränke kaufen.**

(40 seconds)

(t) Question number four.

The group leader also tells you about the programme for the afternoon.

What must you do this afternoon? Write **two** things.

(f)   **Heute Nachmittag treffen wir uns alle um 2.00 Uhr im Gemeinschaftsraum. Jeder soll sich kurz vorstellen, Name, Wohnort, usw. und ein wenig über sein Heimatland erzählen. Und das soll natürlich auf Deutsch sein!**

(40 seconds)

(t) Question number five.

During the week you will be working in pairs. The leader sets you a task for the following day.

What is the task? Write **two** things.

(f)   **Ihr beide werdet zusammen arbeiten. Morgen geht ihr auf die Straße. Ihr macht eine Umfrage. Ihr sollt zwanzig verschiedene Leute fragen, was sie für die Umwelt tun.**

(40 seconds)

(t) Question number six.

You make plans for the free time you have in the early evening.

What do your friends suggest? Write **two** things.

(f) or
(m)   **Wir haben heute so lange herumgesessen. Wir müssen unbedingt an die frische Luft. Unterwegs vom Bahnhof habe ich nicht weit von hier ein schönes Freibad gesehen. Wie wär's, wenn wir dahin gehen? Danach können wir uns vielleicht noch dieses Stadtviertel ansehen.**

(40 seconds)

(t) Question number seven.

At the meal, Matti, one of your friends, tells you why he is at the summer school.

Why is Matti here? Write **two** things.

(m)   **Ich bin hier, um mein Deutsch zu verbessern. Ich suche zur Zeit eine Stelle als Verkäufer bei einer Exportfirma in Helsinki. Sprachkenntnisse sind für solche Stellen besonders wichtig.**

(40 seconds)

(t) Question number eight.

Also at your table is Janna, a girl from Prague in the Czech Republic. She tells you about the course she was on last summer.

Why did she enjoy the course? Write **two** things.

(f)   **Letztes Jahr habe ich an einem Sommerkurs in Frankreich teilgenommen. Das war toll. Ich habe junge Leute aus ganz Europa kennengelernt. Am Ende waren wir alle feste Freunde und wir schreiben uns immer noch.**

(40 seconds)

(t) Question number nine.

Matti asks Janna about Prague.

What does he ask Janna?

(m) **Ich war vor vier Jahren als Schüler in Prag. Was hat sich dort in der Zwischenzeit geändert?**

(40 seconds)

(t) Question number ten.

Janna talks about the changes that have taken place in Prague.

What does she say? Write **three** things.

(f) **Es kommen jetzt viel mehr Touristen als früher aus Westeuropa und auch aus den USA. Die Stadt verdient ganz schön viel daran, aber die Straßen in der Stadtmitte sind jetzt leider immer voll von Autos und Reisebussen.**

(40 seconds)

(t) Question number eleven.

After the evening meal, one of the Finnish boys, Järmo, decides he does not want to go out.

What is he complaining about? Write **two** things.

(m) **Ich glaube, ich bleibe heute Abend lieber hier im Haus. Nach meiner langen Reise fühle ich mich total fertig. Mein ganzer Körper tut mir weh. Ich lege mich ins Bett, dann bin ich morgen hoffentlich wieder fit.**

(40 seconds)

(t) Question number twelve.

Matti has a good idea.

What does he suggest to Järmo?

(m) **Hör mal, Järmo. Wir gehen direkt zum Freibad. Wir bleiben höchstens eine Stunde im Wasser. Dann setzen wir uns ins Café am Eingang. Wenn du dich besser fühlst, kannst du uns dort treffen.**

(40 seconds)

(t) End of test.

You now have 5 minutes to look over your answers.

[END OF TRANSCRIPT]

1998
TUESDAY, 26 MAY
1.00 PM – 1.30 PM
(APPROX)

GERMAN
STANDARD GRADE
Credit Level

Listening

Instructions to the Candidate

When you are told to do so, open your paper.

You will hear a number of short items in German. You will hear each item twice, then you will have time to write your answer.

Write your answers, **in English**, in the **separate** answer book provided.

You may take notes as you are listening to the German, but only in your answer book.

You may **not** use a German dictionary.

You are not allowed to leave the examination room until the end of the test.

Marks

During the summer you spend two weeks at an international summer school for young people in Munich.

Während des Sommers besuchst du zwei Wochen lang eine internationale Sommerschule für Jugendliche in München.

1. When you arrive, you meet two fellow students.
   How did they travel to the summer school? Write **two** things. (2)

   *   *   *   *   *

2. You all go to the reception desk, where you are given some information.
   What information are you given? Write **three** things. (3)

   *   *   *   *   *

3. You are told to come to the hall at 11.00 am. The group leader tells you about arrangements for meals and snacks.
   What does she tell you? Write **three** things. (3)

   *   *   *   *   *

4. The group leader also tells you about the programme for the afternoon.
   What must you do this afternoon? Write **two** things. (2)

   *   *   *   *   *

5. During the week you will be working in pairs. The leader sets you a task for the following day.
   What is the task? Write **two** things. (2)

   *   *   *   *   *

6. You make plans for the free time you have in the early evening.
   What do your friends suggest? Write **two** things. (2)

   *   *   *   *   *

7. At the meal, Matti, one of your friends, tells you why he is at the summer school.
   Why is Matti here? Write **two** things. (2)

   *   *   *   *   *

Marks

8. Also at your table is Janna, a girl from Prague in the Czech Republic. She tells you about the course she was on last summer.

Why did she enjoy the course? Write **two** things. **(2)**

* * * * *

9. Matti asks Janna about Prague.

What does he ask Janna? **(1)**

* * * * *

10. Janna talks about the changes that have taken place in Prague.

What does she say? Write **three** things. **(3)**

* * * * *

11. After the evening meal, one of the Finnish boys, Järmo, decides he does not want to go out.

What is he complaining about? Write **two** things. **(2)**

* * * * *

12. Matti has a good idea. What does he suggest to Järmo? **(1)**

* * * * *

Total (25)

[END OF QUESTION PAPER]

1998
TUESDAY, 26 MAY
2.50 PM – 3.50 PM

GERMAN
STANDARD GRADE
Credit Level
(Optional Paper)
Writing

The following young people were asked about their summer holiday plans.

Im Juni fahre ich nach Dänemark. Ich verbringe zwei Wochen dort. Ich habe vor, in Jugendherbergen zu übernachten. Ohne Eltern! Das wird echt super sein.

Konrad, 16 Jahre

Dieses Jahr fliege ich zum ersten Mal mit meinen Eltern in die Türkei. Es soll unheimlich warm sein und ich hoffe, den ganzen Tag am Strand zu faulenzen. Leider wird mein Vater Volleyball und Tennis spielen, und meine Mutti wird bestimmt wandern gehen. Sport und Wandern mag ich nicht.

Ramona, 15 Jahre

Im August fahre ich mit meinen Freunden an die Nordsee. Dort verbringen wir fünf Tage. Wir fahren jedes Jahr an denselben Ort und treffen Freunde von vorigen Jahren. Mit meinen Freunden verstehe ich mich gut. Das ist für mich der ideale Urlaub.

Jens, 17 Jahre

Dieses Jahr bleibe ich daheim. Ich möchte aber Tagesausflüge machen, denn es gibt viele schöne Städte und Dörfer in der Umgebung. Zu Hause kann man sich auch gut erholen.

Hannelore, 16 Jahre

Now it's your turn!

Here are some questions you may wish to consider. You do not have to use all of them, and you are free to include other relevant ideas.

* Where do you usually go on holiday?
* What do you plan to do this year?
* Are you going away or staying at home?
* How will you spend the time?
* With whom?
* Where?

Write about 200 words **in German**. You may use a German dictionary.

[END OF QUESTION PAPER]

1999
WEDNESDAY, 26 MAY
10.25 AM – 11.25 AM

GERMAN
STANDARD GRADE
Credit Level
Reading

Instructions to the Candidate

When you are told to do so, open your paper and write your answers **in English** in the **separate** answer book provided.

You may use a German dictionary.

Marks

Your pen friend has sent you a magazine to read.

1. Two young people write about their plans for the future.

Amos, 18

Ich bin Jude. Nach dem Abitur möchte ich eine Zeitlang in Israel leben, um die Sprache zu lernen.

Das ganze Leben in Israel zu verbringen, kann ich mir aber nicht vorstellen, denn dann müßte ich wie alle jungen Männer dort drei Jahre zur Armee. Davor habe ich große Angst.

(a) What is Amos' plan for the future? Write **one** thing. **(1)**

(b) What problem does he foresee? Write **one** thing. **(1)**

Laura, 15

Ich interessiere mich sehr für Mode. Später möchte ich gerne in einem Modehaus arbeiten. Models wie Naomi Campbell sind heutzutage weltberühmt und verdienen viel Geld. Aber wenn man einen Unfall hat und sich etwas am Gesicht verändert, dann ist alles aus.

(c) What is Laura's plan for the future? Write **one** thing. **(1)**

(d) What possible problem does she foresee? Write **one** thing. **(1)**

Marks

2. These two young people write about their hobbies.

Terley, 14

Früher war's doch so: Die Mädchen haben Volleyball gespielt, die Jungs Fußball. Aber Skaten, das tun sogar Leute, die 30 oder 50 Jahre alt sind.

Inline-Skaten überwindet die Grenzen zwischen den Geschlechtern und den Generationen, das finde ich toll. Deshalb wird es noch lange wichtig bleiben, anders als andere Trends, die schnell wieder vorbei sind.

(*a*)   What appeals to Terley about her inline-skating? Write **two** things.   **(2)**

Für viele meiner Freunde ist es wichtig, ein schnelles Auto zu haben. Ich bin aber für Radfahren.   In zwei bis drei Jahren kostet der Liter Benzin 5 Mark—aber Luft für die Reifen wird es dann immer noch umsonst geben, genau wie die Muskelkraft meiner Beine.   Viele Leute um mich interessieren sich für die Umwelt überhaupt nicht. Mit ihren Autos verpesten sie die Luft. Radfahren ist umweltfreundlich.

Dennis, 17

(*b*)   Dennis prefers cycling to driving a car. What advantages does the bike have over the car? Write **two** things.   **(2)**

Marks

3. The magazine asks: What would you take with you on a desert island?

Ich muß Post von meinen Freunden kriegen. Also ist ein Briefkasten ganz wichtig. Und weil ich viel Zeit vor dem Computer verbringe, kommt der auch mit. Meistens spiele ich daran, ab und zu arbeite ich auch. Falls ich Langeweile haben sollte, gibt es ja noch E-Mail.

Zemian

Mein Kuscheltier, einen kleinen Gorilla, nehme ich auf jeden Fall mit. Wenn ich schon meine Freunde zu Hause lassen muß, habe ich ihn wenigstens dabei. Ich benötige auch mindestens eine Tonne Schokolade. Schokolade soll ja glücklich machen. Ich werde mal ausprobieren, ob das stimmt.

Adeleke

Nichts läuft für mich ohne Fernseher. Beim Fernsehen kann ich mich entspannen. Actionfilme lenken mich ab. Zusätzlich brauche ich einen Sportplatz. Meine Gesundheit ist mir sehr wichtig.

Martin

Ein paar Bücher stecke ich in den Rucksack. Ich würde viel Zeit haben, und Bücher bringen mich immer auf neue Ideen. Auf gar keinen Fall würde ich einen Fernseher mitnehmen—ich nehme lieber ein Paddelboot mit, um wieder von der Insel wegzukommen.

Arthur

Each person has chosen two items to take with them:

Zemian—letter box and computer; Adeleke—cuddly toy and chocolate; Martin—TV and sports ground; Arthur—books and canoe.

Why have they chosen these items? Write **one** reason for each choice.

(8)

Marks

4. A girl called Nicola writes to Claudia, the magazine's agony aunt, about a problem.

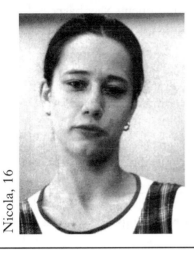

Nicola, 16

Liebe Claudia,
Ich bekomme im Monat nur zehn Mark Taschengeld, aber ich muß jede Woche das Bad und die Küche putzen und in allen Räumen staubsaugen. Wenn ich schlecht saubermache, werden mir fünf Mark abgezogen. Ich helfe aber auch freiwillig im Haushalt, mache Frühstück, hänge die Wäsche auf, usw. Meine Freundinnen bekommen viel mehr Taschengeld und müssen nicht soviel helfen. Das finde ich ungerecht.

(*a*) Why is Nicola unhappy about getting 10 Marks as pocket money? Write **three** things.

(3)

Claudia has some general advice about pocket money.

Liebe Nicola,
Ich stimme Dir zu. Ein Teenager sollte Taschengeld bekommen, ohne dafür arbeiten zu müssen. Taschengeld ist wichtig. Dadurch lernt man, verantwortlich mit Geld umzugehen. Natürlich ist es auch in Ordnung, daß Eltern von ihren Kindern Hilfe im Haushalt erwarten. Aber das sollte das Taschengeld nicht beeinflussen.

(*b*) What does Claudia say about pocket money in general? Write **four** things.

(4)

Marks

Claudia suggests what Nicola should do.

Vielleicht solltest Du zuerst mit den Eltern Deiner Freundinnen, Nachbarn oder Verwandten reden, mit denen Du Dich gut verstehst und die die Taschengeldfrage nicht so eng sehen wie Deine Eltern.

Hör Dich in Deinem Freundeskreis um, wieviel Taschengeld die anderen bekommen und was sie davon bezahlen müssen. Manche Jugendliche bekommen sehr viel Taschengeld, aber mit dem Geld müssen sie selbst Kleidung, Schulsachen und Ähnliches kaufen.

Überleg Dir Deine Argumente noch mal gut und besprich das Ganze dann mit Deinen Eltern. Wenn Du ruhig und freundlich mit ihnen sprichst, könnt Ihr sicher einen Kompromiß finden.

(c)   What does she suggest Nicola should do? Write **three** things   **(3)**

Total (26)

[*END OF QUESTION PAPER*]

GERMAN
STANDARD GRADE
Credit Level
Listening Transcript

Transcript—Credit Level

Instructions to reader(s):

For each item, read the English **once**, then read the German **twice**, with an interval of 7 seconds between the two readings. On completion of the second reading, pause for the length of time indicated in brackets after each item, to allow the candidates to write their answers.

Where special arrangements have been agreed in advance to allow the reading of the material, those sections marked **(f)** should be read by a female speaker and those marked **(m)** by a male: those sections marked **(t)** should be read by the teacher.

(t) You are staying with your pen friend, Heike, in Munich. You have each bought a one-week season ticket to allow you to travel around Germany by train.

(f) or (m) **Du wohnst bei deiner Brieffreundin Heike in München. Ihr habt beide eine Wochenkarte gekauft, mit der ihr in ganz Deutschland mit dem Zug fahren könnt.**

(t) Question number one.

Heike suggests where you could travel to first.

Where does she suggest you go? Why does she suggest this?

(f) **Ich schlage vor, wir fahren zuerst direkt in den Norden. Ich habe eine Tante dort, wo wir übers Wochenende bleiben könnten.**

(40 seconds)

(t) Question number two.

On the train you meet a German couple. They tell you they are travelling to Cologne.

Why are they going there? What must they do when they get to Cologne?

(f) or (m) **Wir steigen in Köln aus. Eine Freundin hat uns zu ihrer Geburtstagsfeier eingeladen. Wir müssen ein Geschenk für sie kaufen. In Köln gibt es gute Einkaufsmöglichkeiten.**

(40 seconds)

(t) Question number three.

The train arrives in Cologne.

What is Heike going to do? What does she suggest you do?

(f) **Hör mal, hast du Hunger? Der Zug hat hier in Köln fünfzehn Minuten Aufenthalt. Wie wär's, wenn ich schnell aussteige und hier am Bahnhof etwas zu essen besorge? Es ist besser, wenn du hier im Zug beim Gepäck bleibst.**

(40 seconds)

(t) Question number four.

Later that day you arrive in Lübeck.

How will you and Heike get to her aunt's house? Write **two** things.

What does Heike suggest you do before you go there?

(f)   Mein Onkel arbeitet hier in der Stadtmitte. Er kommt mit dem Auto erst um 17.20 Uhr und holt uns vom Bahnhof ab. Wir haben also fast zwei Stunden Zeit, um uns die Altstadt anzusehen.

(*40 seconds*)

(t) Question number five.

Later in the evening, Heike's uncle suggests what you could do at the weekend.

What does he suggest? Write **two** things.

(m)   Wir haben ein Wochenendhäuschen an der Nordsee. Habt ihr Lust, mit uns das Wochenende dort zu verbringen? Das Haus liegt direkt am Strand, und bei diesem schönen Wetter könnt ihr im Meer baden.

(*40 seconds*)

(t) Question number six.

During the weekend, Heike says she has a problem.

What is her problem?

What does her uncle suggest? Write **two** things.

(f)   — Ich habe mir einen ordentlichen Sonnenbrand geholt. Ich brauche unbedingt etwas dagegen.

(m)   — Oh, du, das sieht aber schlimm aus. Ich fahre dich schnell zum Arzt. Er wird dir bestimmt eine Salbe verschreiben.

(*40 seconds*)

(t) Question number seven.

The next day, Heike's uncle suggests going on a trip.

What are you going to do? Write **three** things.

(m)   Wollen wir heute einen Ausflug machen? Die dänische Grenze ist nicht weit von hier. Wir können uns also ein bißchen von Dänemark ansehen und auf der Rückfahrt die Ostseeküste entlang fahren. In einem schönen, alten Restaurant können wir zu Abend essen.

(*40 seconds*)

(t) Question number eight.

You discuss what to do the following day. Heike has friends in Berlin. She wants to visit them.

What does she tell you about her friends? Write **two** things.

(f)   **Wir können in Berlin bei meinen Freundinnen Ulla und Susanne übernachten. Ulla arbeitet in einem großen Kaufhaus in der Stadt. Susanne ist bei einer amerikanischen Firma in der Exportabteilung.**

(40 seconds)

(t) Question number nine.

Heike tells you where her friends live.

What does she say about their flat and about the district where they live?

(f)   **Sie haben eine schöne Wohnung in einem alten Gebäude. Es liegt ziemlich weit draußen und es ist ganz ruhig dort, mit vielen Bäumen und einem kleinen See in der Nähe.**

(40 seconds)

(t) Question number ten.

On Tuesday you will be going to Nürnberg on the night train.

Why is the night train a good idea? Write **two** things.

(f)   **Am Dienstag können wir mit dem Nachtzug nach Nürnberg fahren. Wir können im Zug übernachten und dabei Geld sparen. Dann haben wir den ganzen Tag, uns die Stadt anzusehen.**

(40 seconds)

(t) Question number eleven.

Heike makes a suggestion for the rest of the week.

What does she suggest? Write **two** things.

(f)   **Am Bahnhof in Nürnberg kann man Fahrräder mieten. Von Nürnberg nach München sind es nur 120 Kilometer. Wenn wir mit dem Rad langsam nach München zurückfahren, sind wir am Wochenende wieder zu Hause.**

(40 seconds)

(t) End of test.

You now have 5 minutes to look over your answers.

[END OF TRANSCRIPT]

GERMAN
STANDARD GRADE
Credit Level
Listening

Instructions to the Candidate

When you are told to do so, open your paper.

You will hear a number of short items in German. You will hear each item twice, then you will have time to write your answer.

Write your answers, **in English**, in the **separate** answer book provided.

You may take notes as you are listening to the German, but only in your answer book.

You may **not** use a German dictionary.

You are not allowed to leave the examination room until the end of the test.

Marks

You are staying with your pen friend, Heike, in Munich. You have each bought a one-week season ticket to allow you to travel around Germany by train.

Du wohnst bei deiner Brieffreundin Heike in München. Ihr habt beide eine Wochenkarte gekauft, mit der ihr in ganz Deutschland mit dem Zug fahren könnt.

1. Heike suggests where you could travel to first.
   (a) Where does she suggest you go? **(1)**
   (b) Why does she suggest this? **(1)**

*   *   *   *   *

2. On the train you meet a German couple. They tell you they are travelling to Cologne.
   (a) Why are they going there? **(1)**
   (b) What must they do when they get to Cologne? **(1)**

*   *   *   *   *

3. The train arrives in Cologne.
   (a) What is Heike going to do? **(1)**
   (b) What does she suggest you do? **(1)**

*   *   *   *   *

Marks

4. Later that day you arrive in Lübeck.
   (*a*) How will you and Heike get to her aunt's house? Write **two** things. **(2)**
   (*b*) What does Heike suggest you do before you go there? **(1)**

*   *   *   *   *

5. Later in the evening, Heike's uncle suggests what you could do at the weekend.
   What does he suggest? Write **two** things. **(2)**

*   *   *   *   *

6. During the weekend, Heike says she has a problem.
   (*a*) What is her problem? **(1)**
   (*b*) What does her uncle suggest? Write **two** things. **(2)**

*   *   *   *   *

7. The next day, Heike's uncle suggests going on a trip.
   What are you going to do? Write **three** things. **(3)**

*   *   *   *   *

8. You discuss what to do the following day. Heike has friends in Berlin. She wants to visit them.
   What does she tell you about her friends? Write **two** things. **(2)**

*   *   *   *   *

9. Heike tells you where her friends live.
   What does she say:
   (*a*) about their flat? **(1)**
   (*b*) about the district where they live? **(1)**

*   *   *   *   *

10. On Tuesday you will be going to Nürnberg on the night train.
    Why is the night train a good idea? Write **two** things. **(2)**

*   *   *   *   *

11. Heike makes a suggestion for the rest of the week.
    What does she suggest? Write **two** things **(2)**

*   *   *   *   *

[END OF QUESTION PAPER]

Total (25)

1999
THURSDAY, 27 MAY
2.45 PM – 3.45 PM

GERMAN
STANDARD GRADE
Credit Level
(Optional Paper)
Writing

These young people were asked to write about a typical weekend **and** also a special weekend they enjoyed sometime in the past.

Am Samstagvormittag muß ich bis 11 Uhr in die Schule gehen. Danach treffe ich mich mit meinen Eltern in der Stadtmitte. Sonntags faulenze ich in meinem Zimmer. Vor zwei Wochen haben wir das Wochenende in den Bergen verbracht. Dort sind wir wandern gegangen.

Martin

Samstags arbeite ich bei einer Friseurin. Ich wasche Haare und koche Kaffee. Am Samstagabend gehe ich zum Jugendzentrum mit Freundinnen.

Im Oktober bin ich mit der Schule nach London gefahren. Das hat viel Spaß gemacht.

Miriam

Normalerweise verbringe ich das Wochenende mit Freunden. Wir gehen entweder in die Stadtmitte einkaufen oder ins Kino. Sonntags ist nicht viel los. Meistens gehe ich in die Kirche und dann mache ich meine Hausaufgaben. Neulich haben wir einen Naturpark besucht, wo man die Tiere füttern darf. Das fand ich einfach toll!

Ramona

Jedes Wochenende ist es immer dasselbe. Samstags muß ich mit meinem Vater zum Supermarkt fahren. Dort kaufen wir für die Woche ein. Nachmittags spiele ich Fußball und abends kommen meine Freunde bei mir vorbei. Vor zwei Wochen bin ich mit meiner Klasse aufs Land gefahren. Wir haben zwei Nächte in einer Jugendherberge verbracht.

Kurt

Now it's your turn!

Here are some questions you may wish to consider. You do not have to use all of them, and you are free to include other relevant ideas.

A typical weekend

* What do you usually do at the weekend? Do you do the same things every weekend? What do you enjoy doing most at the weekend?

* Do you have a weekend job?

A special weekend

* Where did you go? Who did you go with? What did you do?

Write about 200 words **in German**. You may use a German dictionary.

NATIONAL
QUALIFICATIONS
2000

WEDNESDAY, 7 JUNE
10.25 AM – 11.25 AM

GERMAN
STANDARD GRADE
Credit Level
Reading

Instructions to the Candidate

When you are told to do so, open your paper and write your answers **in English** in the **separate** answer book provided.

You may use a German dictionary.

Marks

Your German pen friend has sent you a magazine.

1. In this article four young people write about anxieties they have.

> Meine Eltern sagen mir fast jeden Tag, das Wichtigste ist, daß ich ein gutes Abitur mache. Eine Zeitlang hatte ich überhaupt keine Lust auf Schule und habe wochenlang keine Hausaufgaben gemacht.
>
> Barbara

(*a*) How do Barbara's parents make her feel anxious about school?   1

(*b*) What effect did this have on her? Write **two** things.   2

> Ich mache mir wegen meines Aussehens den totalen Streß. Ich vergleiche mich dauernd mit den anderen und frage mich, wie sie mich finden. Nach außen tue ich dann total cool, aber innerlich bin ich ganz unsicher. Zu Hause finde ich mich okay, aber sobald ich rausgehe, fängt es an, „O Gott, wie sehe ich aus?"
>
> Axel

(*c*) In what ways does Axel worry about his appearance? Write **two** things.   2

Marks

Ich habe immer Angst, wenn ich einen Jungen mit nach Hause bringe, wie meine Eltern reagieren werden. Meine Eltern meinen, der Junge muß aus der gleichen Sozialgruppe kommen wie ich.

Julie

(*d*) How do her parents' attitudes to boyfriends cause Julie stress? Write **two** things.

2

Für die Zukunft gibt es so viele Möglichkeiten! Aber was ist, wenn ich den falschen Beruf wähle und das erst mit 25 Jahren merke? Es ist beängstigend, plötzlich vieles selber machen zu müssen.

Peter

(*e*) How do thoughts about the future cause Peter stress? Write **two** things.

2

2. These young people were asked when they last told a lie.

Wann hast du zuletzt GELOGEN?

Vorgestern wollte ich mich mit meinen Freunden treffen. Es gab ein bißchen Krach mit meinen Eltern, weil ich abends so oft weg war. Deshalb haben sie mir verboten, schon wieder auszugehen. Ich habe einfach erzählt, daß ich etwas Wichtiges abholen mußte, und ich bin trotzdem ausgegangen.

Barbara

(a) Why did Barbara tell her parents a lie? Write **two** things.　2

(b) What did she tell them?　1

Ich habe vorletzte Woche einen netten Jungen getroffen. Ich habe gelogen und ihm gesagt, daß ich keinen Freund hätte, weil ich ihn besser kennenlernen wollte. Wir haben uns dann oft abends gesehen und ich mußte ihm dann doch sagen, daß ich einen anderen Freund hätte.

Monika

(c) What lie did Monika tell the boy?　1

(d) Why did she tell this lie?　1

Meine Mutter wollte mir zum Geburtstag eine neue Gitarre kaufen. Ich habe meiner Mutter vorgelogen, daß die Gitarre 100DM mehr kostet, als sie erwartet hat. So hatte ich dann Geld übrig, um mir neue Kleidung zu kaufen. Ich spiele in einer Band und muß natürlich schick aussehen!

Siggi

(e) What lie did Siggi tell his mother?　1

(f) Why did he tell this lie? Write **two** things.　2

Marks

3. Two young people talk about things in their lives which give them pleasure and purpose.

(*Bernhard works voluntarily for the Red Cross.*)

Bernhard ist achtzehn und im letzten Schuljahr. Seit zwei Jahren arbeitet er dreimal im Monat als Helfer bei dem Roten Kreuz. Das war immer sein Traum, seitdem er selbst nach einem Unfall mit einem Rettungswagen ins Krankenhaus gebracht wurde.

Bernhard sagt: „Es gibt viele Menschen, die unsere Hilfe brauchen. Es macht mir große Freude, solchen Leuten zu helfen. Ich bringe zum Beispiel eine körperbehinderte Dame einmal im Monat ins Theater. In der Pause bleibe ich bei ihr und wir besprechen den Inhalt.

Ich habe immer das Gefühl, daß ich auch von ihr sehr viel bekomme. Ich sehe jetzt viele Dinge und meine eigenen Probleme ganz anders.“

(*a*) What motivated Bernhard to be a volunteer with the Red Cross? **1**

(*b*) What examples does he give of his work? Write **two** things. **2**

(*c*) How does Bernhard feel he himself benefits? **2**

Marks

(*Sabine is learning Japanese at school.*)

Sabine ist siebzehn und geht in die siebte Klasse in einem Gymnasium. Seit zwei Jahren lernt sie in der Schule Japanisch. „Die japanische Kultur hat mich schon immer fasziniert, sie ist völlig anders als die europäische. Es ist schon ein gutes Gefühl, etwas zu können, was nicht jeder kann.

Man bekommt viel mehr Verständnis für andere Menschen, wenn man sich auch mit ihrer Sprache und ihrer Kultur beschäftigt. Von unserer japanischen Lehrerin lernen wir viel über Jugendliche in Japan, daß man dort viel strengere Disziplin in der Schule hat, als wir.“

(*d*)   Why has Sabine chosen to learn Japanese? Write **two** things.   2

(*e*)   What does she feel she gets out of it? Write **two** things.   2

Total (26)

[*END OF QUESTION PAPER*]

Transcript—Credit Level

> **Instructions to reader(s):**
>
> For each item, read the English **once**, then read the German **three times**, with an interval of 5 seconds between the readings. On completion of the third reading, pause for the length of time indicated in brackets after each item, to allow the candidates to write their answers.
>
> Where special arrangements have been agreed in advance to allow the reading of the material, those sections marked **(f)** should be read by a female speaker and those marked **(m)** by a male: those sections marked **(t)** should be read by the teacher.

(t) You are travelling to Austria to go skiing. You arrive at the station in Innsbruck. A ski instructor from your hotel is waiting to collect you.

(f) or (m)   **Du fährst nach Österreich zum Skilaufen. Du kommst in Innsbruck an. Ein Skilehrer vom Hotel ist am Bahnhof, um dich abzuholen.**

(t) Question number one.

He asks you about your journey.

What does he ask you? Write **two** things.

(m)   **Willkommen in Innsbruck! Das war eine lange Reise von Schottland! Wann bist du von zu Hause weggefahren? Hast du in München übernachtet?**

(40 seconds)

(t) Question number two.

He explains why you won't be going straight to the hotel.

Why do you have to wait?

(m)   **Wir müssen leider noch zehn Minuten hier warten. Es kommen noch Gäste mit dem nächsten Zug.**

(40 seconds)

(t) Question number three.

You are at the hotel reception.

What does the receptionist ask you to do?

What does she tell you about your room? Write **two** things.

(f)   **Guten Tag! Möchten Sie bitte dieses Formular ausfüllen?**
Sie bekommen ein Einzelzimmer, nicht wahr? Das ist ein Nichtraucherzimmer im zweiten Stock.

(40 seconds)

(t) Question number four.

The receptionist tells you about meal arrangements.

What does she tell you about:

breakfast?

lunch?

your evening meal?

(f)   **Zum Frühstück gehen Sie bitte ins Gebäude direkt nebenan. Nach dem Frühstück können Sie Lunchpakete von der Küche abholen. Und zum Abendessen heute gibt es ein traditionelles Gericht aus Österreich.**

(40 seconds)

(t) Question number five.

The receptionist gives you instructions about the evening.

What will you be doing this evening?

What must you bring with you? Write **two** things.

(f)   **Alle Skigäste sollten sich um acht Uhr unten im Keller treffen. Wir werden Skistiefel und Skier anprobieren. Bringen Sie bitte dicke Socken und ein Foto für Ihren Skipaß mit!**

(40 seconds)

(t) Question number six.

That evening you chat to the ski instructor. He tells you about the types of people he meets in his job.

What does he say about the older people he meets?

What does he say about the younger people he meets?

(m)   **Ich komme mit den älteren Gästen sehr gut aus. Sie sind meistens sehr höflich und freundlich mir gegenüber. Die jüngeren Gäste lernen aber viel schneller skifahren!**

(40 seconds)

(t) Question number seven.

He tells you about a trip to Salzburg which is on offer on Saturday.

What will you do in Salzburg:

in the morning?

and in the afternoon?

(m)   **Es gibt am Samstag einen Ausflug nach Salzburg. Man hat die Gelegenheit, morgens die Sehenswürdigkeiten anzusehen. Nachmittags kann man einen Einkaufsbummel durch das alte Stadtzentrum machen. Da hat man eine große Auswahl an Geschäften.**

(40 seconds)

(t) Question number eight.

A German lady gives her opinion of the trip to Salzburg.

Why is she not interested in the trip? Write **two** things.

(f) Ach, das interessiert mich nicht. Ich wohne sowieso in einer Großstadt, und ich finde alle Städte gleich langweilig. Ich würde lieber einen Spaziergang auf dem Land machen.

(40 seconds)

(t) Question number nine.

The instructor tells you about an incident last week.

What happened? Write **three** things.

(m) Letzte Woche haben wir einen fünfzehnjährigen Jungen oben auf dem Berg verloren. Wir haben stundenlang gesucht und konnten ihn nicht finden. Er ist dann vier Stunden später unten angekommen.

(40 seconds)

(t) Question number ten.

He tells you what state the person was in.

What state was he in? Write **two** things.

(m) Als er endlich ankam, waren wir alle sehr froh, ihn zu sehen. Er zitterte vor Angst und konnte kaum mehr gehen.

(40 seconds)

(t) Question number eleven.

Your instructor has visited Scotland. He talks about Scotland and Austria.

Why does he like Scotland so much?

Why does he like Austria?

(m) In Schottland ist man nie sehr weit vom Meer entfernt. Das finde ich toll!
Hier in Österreich sind die Berge viel höher und der Schnee bleibt deswegen viel länger liegen. Das ist natürlich gut!

(40 seconds)

(t) End of test.

Now look over your answers.

[END OF TRANSCRIPT]

NATIONAL
QUALIFICATIONS
2000

WEDNESDAY, 7 JUNE
1.30 PM – 2.00 PM
(APPROX)

GERMAN
STANDARD GRADE
Credit Level
Listening

Instructions to the Candidate

When you are told to do so, open your paper.

You will hear a number of short items in German. You will hear each item three times, then you will have time to write your answer.

Write your answers, **in English**, in the **separate** answer book provided.

You may take notes as you are listening to the German, but only in your answer book.

You may **not** use a German dictionary.

You are not allowed to leave the examination room until the end of the test.

Marks

You are travelling to Austria to go skiing. You arrive at the station in Innsbruck. A ski instructor from your hotel is waiting to collect you.

Du fährst nach Österreich zum Skilaufen. Du kommst in Innsbruck an. Ein Skilehrer vom Hotel ist am Bahnhof, um dich abzuholen.

1. He asks you about your journey.

   What does he ask you? Write **two** things.   2

   *   *   *   *   *

2. He explains why you won't be going straight to the hotel.

   Why do you have to wait?   1

   *   *   *   *   *

3. You are at the hotel reception.
   (*a*)   What does the receptionist ask you to do?   1
   (*b*)   What does she tell you about your room? Write **two** things.   2

   *   *   *   *   *

4. The receptionist tells you about meal arrangements.

   What does she tell you about:
   (*a*)   breakfast?
   (*b*)   lunch?
   (*c*)   your evening meal?   3

   *   *   *   *   *

5. The receptionist gives you instructions about the evening.
   (*a*)   What will you be doing this evening?   1
   (*b*)   What must you bring with you? Write **two** things.   2

   *   *   *   *   *

6. That evening you chat to the ski instructor. He tells you about the types of people he meets in his job.
   (*a*)   What does he say about the older people he meets?   1
   (*b*)   What does he say about the younger people he meets?   1

   *   *   *   *   *

Marks

7. He tells you about a trip to Salzburg which is on offer on Saturday.
What will you do in Salzburg:

    (*a*)   in the morning?   **1**

    (*b*)   in the afternoon?   **1**

*   *   *   *   *

8. A German lady gives her opinion of the trip to Salzburg.
Why is she not interested in the trip? Write **two** things.   **2**

*   *   *   *   *

9. The instructor tells you about an incident last week.
What happened? Write **three** things.   **3**

*   *   *   *   *

10. He tells you what state the person was in.
What state was he in? Write **two** things.   **2**

*   *   *   *   *

11. Your instructor has visited Scotland. He talks about Scotland and Austria.

    (*a*)   Why does he like Scotland so much?   **1**

    (*b*)   Why does he like Austria?   **1**

*   *   *   *   *

Total (25)

[END OF QUESTION PAPER]

NATIONAL
QUALIFICATIONS
2000

MONDAY, 12 JUNE
2.35 PM – 3.35 PM

GERMAN
STANDARD GRADE
Credit Level
(Additional)
Writing

These young people have written about parties and other celebrations they have.

Carsten

Vor zwei Jahren hatte ich eine Party. Leider klagten die Nachbarn bei der Polizei über den Lärm. Seitdem gehen wir irgendwo essen und danach in die Disko. Dort tanzen wir und hören Musik.

Maren

Letzte Woche war ich von einer Freundin zur Geburtstagsfeier eingeladen. Wir sind zu fünft zuerst ins Kino gegangen und haben uns einen tollen Film angesehen. Danach sind wir zusammen essen gegangen. Es hat Spaß gemacht.

Monika

Zum Geburtstag bleibe ich immer zu Hause. Mit meinen Eltern und Freunden haben wir ein großes Fest. Wir essen alle zusammen und dann hören wir Musik und unterhalten uns.

Fritz

Als ich neulich eine Party gegeben habe, bin ich mit meinem Freund einkaufen gegangen. Wir haben Getränke, Wurst, Chips und Senf gekauft. Wir haben im Garten gegrillt, Gitarre gespielt und gesungen.

What do you do to celebrate? What do your friends do?

Here are some ideas you may wish to consider. You do not have to use all of them, and you are free to include other relevant ideas.

* You could describe a recent celebration. Where did you go? What did you do?

* Do you often go to parties?

* What do you do at parties?

* What do you wear?

Write about 200 words **in German**. You may use a German dictionary.

[END OF QUESTION PAPER]

Printed by Bell & Bain Ltd., Glasgow, Scotland